# PROPHECY
## FOR THE
# GENTILES

## A VERSE-BY-VERSE PROPHECY STUDY

*Obadiah-Jonah-Nahum-Habakkuk*

D0111925

Virtually all Scripture references are quoted from the King James translation of the Holy Bible.

## Prophecy for the Gentiles

Published by The Olive Press, a division of Midnight Call, Inc. West Columbia, SC 29170 U.S.A.


Copy Typists:     Lynn Jeffcoat and Kathy Roland
Copy Editor:      Kimberly Farmer
Layout/Design:    Michelle Kim
Cover Design:     Michelle Kim



Froese, Arno
     Prophecy for the Gentiles
     ISBN #9780937422700

     1. Bible--Prophecy

Printed in the United States of America

The sole purpose of publishing this book is to encourage the readers to surrender and consecrate their lives to Christ.

All funds received from the sale of this book will be used exclusively for the furtherance of the Gospel.

No one associated with this ministry receives a royalty for any of the literature published by Midnight Call Ministries, Inc.

# CONTENTS

# OBADIAH

*Servant of Jehovah*

# OBADIAH

| Book of the Bible | God's Directly Spoken Words (%) | Prophecy %* | Significant Names Listed in Each Book | | | | | | |
|---|---|---|---|---|---|---|---|---|---|
| | | | Judah | Israel | Ephraim | Jerusalem | Zion | Heathen | Samaria |
| Hosea | 93.32 | 56 | 15 | 44 | 37 | 0 | 0 | 0 | 6 |
| Joel | 57.70 | 68 | 6 | 3 | 0 | 6 | 7 | 5 | 0 |
| Amos | 80.95 | 58 | 4 | 30 | 0 | 2 | 2 | 1 | 5 |
| **Obadiah** | 97.69 | 81 | 1 | 1 | 1 | 2 | 2 | 4 | 1 |
| Jonah | 7.39 | 10 | 0 | 0 | 0 | 0 | 0 | 0 | 0 |
| Micah | 44.88 | 70 | 4 | 12 | 0 | 8 | 9 | 1 | 3 |
| Nahum | 40.30 | 74 | 1 | 1 | 0 | 0 | 0 | 0 | 0 |
| Habakkuk | 47.84 | 41 | 0 | 0 | 0 | 0 | 0 | 2 | 0 |
| Zephaniah | 96.92 | 89 | 3 | 4 | 0 | 4 | 2 | 1 | 0 |
| Haggai | 67.61 | 39 | 4 | 0 | 0 | 0 | 0 | 1 | 0 |
| Zechariah | 77.38 | 69 | 22 | 5 | 3 | 41 | 8 | 5 | 0 |
| Malachi | 93.80 | 56 | 3 | 5 | 0 | 2 | 0 | 2 | 0 |

* Percentage of book as prophecy according to *Tim LaHaye Prophecy Study Bible*

## Introduction to Obadiah

From the 12 Minor Prophets, Obadiah is the first who is concerned about the heathen; in particular, the nation of Edom. It may be a strong statement to call Edom, which is Esau, the twin brother of Jacob, heathen, but as we will see in this study, Esau indeed became as one of the heathen, and as a result "shall be cut off forever."

Obadiah is fourth in line of the 12 Prophets, and has the shortest message, yet an extremely powerful one, as we will see.

Virtually all the prophets of the Old Testament have a twofold message:

1) Judgment against those who have transgressed God's law; and

2) Restoration, particularly for one nation, Israel.

We find significant details regarding the reason why judgment had to come. That's what this 21-verse book of Obadiah is about.

What sets Obadiah aside from most of the other prophets is the unique introduction, "The vision of Obadiah." The other prophets make a more direct statement such as, "The word of the Lord came...." What is the difference?

Before we answer that question, let us look at an example in the Book of Daniel. That book is a precise, historic account of real people, kings and nations. Daniel gives the time, places, measurements, names, and geographical boundaries; he reports down-to-earth manifestations. But then about halfway through the book, we read of visions: "Daniel had a dream and visions" (Daniel 7:1). From that point on, the names of kings and nations play a lesser role in relationship to what he actually sees and reports. Daniel passes on visions he has received from God.

We have another example in the last book of the Bible. After the seven churches are revealed, identified by name and geography, we read: "After this I looked, and, behold, a door was opened in heaven: and the first voice which I heard was as it were of a trumpet talking with me; which said, Come up hither, and I will show thee things which must be hereafter. And immediately I was in the spirit: and, behold, a throne was set in heaven, and one sat on the throne" (Revelation 4:1-2).

John begins to write down the things he sees in relationship to eternity. He describes them, as did Daniel, from spiritual perspectives. He writes them as if they were happening at that very moment, yet it would be thousands of years before they would be visibly fulfilled on earth.

The vision of Obadiah in the first place witnesses the pronouncement of judgment upon Edom. Then, it follows with judgment upon the nations of the world. Finally, it deals with the restoration of Israel.

It is helpful to realize that the Hebrew name Obadiah means "Servant of Jehovah" in English. Thus, his name reinforces the truth that he is passing on a message from God.

It is not surprising, therefore, that we find no further identification regarding this man Obadiah. We have no historical evidence as to the date of his birth, the name of his father, or other references which would place him at a certain time in history. We may say he was a nobody, just a mouthpiece of the Lord God. Quite fittingly, his name is "Servant of Jehovah."

# Chapter 1

## Edom Reduced

**Verses 1-2:** "The vision of Obadiah. Thus saith the Lord GOD concerning Edom; We have heard a rumour from the LORD, and an ambassador is sent among the heathen, Arise ye, and let us rise up against her in battle. 2 Behold, I have made thee small among the heathen: thou art greatly despised."

(See) Isaiah 21:11; Ezekiel 25:12-14; Joel 3:19; Malachi 1:4

What does it mean: "an ambassador is sent among the heathen"? It is a prophecy of destruction of the nations of the world during the final confrontation known as the Battle of Armageddon. In other words, all the nations of the world are participants in the opposition against God. It is the Lord God who reveals a clear message addressed to the heathen, relating to the destruction of Edom.

The word "rumour" in the KJV is a poor choice, since the Hebrew word indicates "doctrine," "report" or "tidings." Quite obviously, this is the Lord's doing because Edom is destined to be "greatly despised" among the heathen nations.

## Who Is Edom?

The answer is given in Genesis 36:8: "Esau is Edom." This is important to understand, because Esau is the twin brother of Jacob. The conflict between these two brothers is recorded for us in Genesis 25, in the prophecy addressed to Rebekah, the mother of Jacob and Esau: "And the LORD said unto her, Two nations are in thy womb, and two manner of people shall be separated from thy bowels; and the one people shall be stronger than the other people; and the elder shall serve the younger" (verse 23).

We know from this chapter that Esau sold his birthright to his twin brother Jacob, "...thus Esau despised his birthright" (verse 34). Quite obviously, Esau was a fleshly and earthly-minded person; he wanted his share here and now. He did not care about God's order, nor about the special promises for the firstborn. The fact that Jacob knew the advantage of being the firstborn indicates that Esau knew it as well. But spiritual things did not concern Esau; his aim was to have his belly filled NOW. This man was a realist: he only believed in what he saw, or in this case what he could smell, "And Jacob sod pottage."

Later in history, the Epistle of Jude identifies the spirit of Cain and Balaam, people who were earthly realists: "But these speak evil of those things which they know not: but what they know naturally, as brute beasts, in those things they corrupt themselves. Woe unto them! for they have gone in the way of Cain, and ran greedily after the error of Balaam for reward, and perished in the gainsaying of Core. These are spots in your feasts of charity, when they feast with you, feeding themselves without fear: clouds they are without water, carried about of winds; trees whose fruit withereth, without fruit, twice dead, plucked up by the roots" (verses 10-13). Esau fits into that category.

## Esau versus Jacob

In our day we would probably call Esau the good fellow, the one who minds his own business, who does his own thing: "And the boys grew: and Esau was a cunning hunter, a man of the field; and Jacob was a plain man, dwelling in tents" (Genesis 25:27). Jacob actually looks more like a dishonest person. Even his name means "supplanter" or "deceiver." Jacob himself testified to his mother when she came up with a plan to deceive Isaac, "My father peradventure will feel me, and I shall seem to him as a deceiver; and I shall bring a curse upon me, and not a blessing" (Genesis 27:12). Later we read that Esau, when speaking to his father, reveals the meaning of the name Jacob, "Is not he rightly named Jacob? for he hath supplanted me these two times: he took away my birthright; and, behold, now he hath taken away my blessing" (Genesis 27:36). Note the typical reaction of a sinner, slightly twisting the truth by accusing Jacob, "He took away my birthright," instead of acknowledging, "I despised my birthright."

Reading Jacob's history, we learn that his heart was in the right place. He feared God and did what was pleasing in His sight.

## Jacob the Deceiver

But there was still one problem—the name Jacob, meaning "supplanter" or "deceiver." God had to take care of it. When Jacob returned toward the land of his father with great riches, his wives and 11 sons, Esau his brother was on his way to meet him. Now Jacob is confronted with his name, "deceiver." But again, Jacob did the right thing. Genesis 32:24 reports: "And Jacob was left alone; and there wrestled a man with him until the breaking of the day." Note carefully that Jacob is not wrestling with the man, but the unnamed man with him. What was happening here? God was breaking Jacob's self-will, and Jacob accepted it, which is evident from the words recorded in verse 26: "Let me go, for the day breaketh. And he (Jacob) said, I will not let thee go, except thou bless me." Jacob knew to the very depths of his soul that he could only meet Esau with God on his side—he must have the blessing from heaven.

## Jacob Becomes Israel

Then comes the decisive question, "What is thy name? And he said, Jacob" (Genesis 32:27). With the confession of his name, he surrendered himself; he gives up his old nature. What happens next? "Thy name shall be called no more Jacob, but Israel: for as a prince hast thou power with God and with men, and hast prevailed" (verse 28).

This teaches the clear distinction between Esau, the man of the flesh, and Jacob, the man of the spirit. Jacob tried everything in his power to make amends; he was willing to repent. But of Esau we read, "And Esau hated Jacob" (Genesis 27:41). Later we read in Hebrews 12:17: "For ye know how that afterward, when he would have inherited the blessing, he was rejected: for he found no place of repentance, though he sought it carefully with tears."

With these facts in mind, we understand the words we find in the last book of the Old Testament: "...Was not Esau Jacob's brother? saith the LORD: yet I loved Jacob, And I hated Esau" (Malachi 1:2-3).

## Message to the Proud

Obadiah's vision does not fail to give detailed reasons for God's rejection of Edom:

**Verses 3-4:** "The pride of thine heart hath deceived thee, thou that dwellest in the clefts of the rock, whose habitation is high; that saith in his heart, Who shall bring me down to the ground? 4 Though thou exalt thyself as the eagle, and though thou set thy nest among the stars, thence will I bring thee down, saith the LORD."

(See) 2 Kings 14:7; 2 Chronicles 25:12; Job 20:6-7; Isaiah 14:13-15; Jeremiah 49:16; Amos 9:2; Habakkuk 2:9; Revelation 18:7

The key to Edom's rejection is pride. Pride always deceives. Whether it's personal, family, or national, there should be no room for pride in the heart of a new person in Christ Jesus. The word pride stands out and reminds us of the Church of Laodicea, which proudly proclaimed, "I am rich, and increased with goods, and have need of nothing" (Revelation 3:17).

## Origin of Pride

The origin of pride can be found in the father of lies, the deceiver, the murderer from the beginning: Lucifer. The prophet Isaiah exposes his pride in chapter 14:12-14:

15

"How art thou fallen from heaven, O Lucifer, son of the morning! how art thou cut down to the ground, which didst weaken the nations! For thou hast said in thine heart, I will ascend into heaven, I will exalt my throne above the stars of God: I will sit also upon the mount of the congregation, in the sides of the north: I will ascend above the heights of the clouds; I will be like the most High."

## Edom's Greed

**Verse 5:** "If thieves came to thee, if robbers by night, (how art thou cut off!) would they not have stolen till they had enough? if the grape gatherers came to thee, would they not leave some grapes?"

Edom/Esau wanted it all; there was no room for mercy or compassion for the poor, hungry and downtrodden: "It's me, me and a million times me again." It becomes quite obvious that Esau has reached far beyond God's authorized intentions. His desire to totally destroy Jacob is clearly exposed.

Incidentally, this is a near perfect picture of today's society. It's "me" a million times, insistently proclaimed through the media, particularly in advertising. How to satisfy *self*, how a product can be beneficial to *me* is the key message of virtually all commercials. One might remember a quote from a popular movie, "Greed is good." That is the spirit of Esau.

God exposes the very inner being of Esau:

**Verse 6:** "How are the things of Esau searched out! how are his hidden things sought up!"

Nothing will be spared; everything will be laid open. All the hidden anger, evil and wrath is brought to light. The example is given of a robber who breaks in and steals certain things he wants, but not more. Or how someone who comes to a vineyard to steal, would surely leave some grapes. But not Esau; he wants it all—"Greed is good."

The things he has sown, he will reap:

**Verse 7:** "All the men of thy confederacy have brought thee even to the border: the men that were at peace with thee have deceived thee, and prevailed against thee; they that eat thy bread have laid a wound under thee: there is none understanding in him."

No friendship, confederacy, treaty, or constitution would guarantee peace and prosperity for Edom.

## Esau's Tragedy

The greatest tragedy in Esau's case is that he never changed; he never repented of his original intention: "And Esau hated Jacob because of the blessing wherewith his father blessed him: and Esau said in his heart, The days of mourning for my father are at hand; then will I slay my brother Jacob" (Genesis 27:41). Later, we read in the New Testament: "Lest there be any fornicator, or profane person, as Esau...he found no place of repentance, though he sought it carefully with tears" (Hebrews 12:16-17).

17

## Wisdom Vanishes

**Verses 8-9:** "Shall I not in that day, saith the LORD, even destroy the wise men out of Edom, and understanding out of the mount of Esau? 9 And thy mighty men, O Teman, shall be dismayed, to the end that every one of the mount of Esau may be cut off by slaughter."

(See) Psalm 76:5; Jeremiah 49:22; Amos 2:16; Nahum 3:13

What is the result, when wisdom is lacking and understanding fails? A person is so debased that he sinks to the level of an animal. It is no wonder that the Antichrist is called the beast. No military might, no man of war can save. Esau indeed has become greatly despised among the nations. In plain words, we can say Esau became stupefied; they no longer had the intellectual capacity to function as a civilized society.

## "Thou Shouldest Not Have"

Obadiah's vision does not fail to reveal the smallest details. In reading the following verses, we notice the word "shouldest" appears seven times:

**Verses 10-14:** "For thy violence against thy brother Jacob shame shall cover thee, and thou shalt be cut off for ever. 11 In the day that thou stoodest on the other side, in the day that the strangers carried away captive his forces, and foreigners entered into his gates, and cast lots upon Jerusalem, even thou wast as one of them. 12 But thou shouldest not have looked on the day of thy brother in

18

the day that he became a stranger; neither shouldest thou have rejoiced over the children of Judah in the day of their destruction; neither shouldest thou have spoken proudly in the day of distress. 13 Thou shouldest not have entered into the gate of my people in the day of their calamity; yea, thou shouldest not have looked on their affliction in the day of their calamity, nor have laid hands on their substance in the day of their calamity; 14 Neither shouldest thou have stood in the crossway, to cut off those of his that did escape; neither shouldest thou have delivered up those of his that did remain in the day of distress."

(See) Genesis 27:41; Psalm 137:7; Proverbs 24:17; Ezekiel 35:5, 15; Amos 1:11; Micah 4:11; Nahum 3:10; Malachi 1:4

History identifies Edom as one who supported Nebuchadnezzar, the king of Babylon, in his conquest of Jerusalem: "Even thou wast as one of them."

We realize that it was God's judgment by the hand of Nebuchadnezzar upon Jerusalem, but Esau-Edom should have remembered that Jacob-Israel was his brother. That was sufficient reason not to rejoice in the destructive judgment that came upon Judah. While the destruction was not executed by Esau, yet he was counted as "one of them."

1. Esau despised Jacob as a stranger.
2. He rejoiced in the destruction of Judah.
3. He proudly spoke against Jacob.
4. He even participated in the victory march against Jerusalem.

5. He took of the spoils of war.

6. He hindered the escape of the remnant.

7. And Esau became a traitor to his own brother, because he "delivered up those of his that did remain in the day of distress."

We note again the word proud: "Neither shouldest thou have spoken proudly in the day of distress." When reading these few verses, one senses the diabolical hatred of Esau for his brother Jacob. He not only became an enemy and rejoiced proudly against Judah, but participated in stealing the blessings from Jacob: "laid hands on their substance." Even worse, those who escaped the slaughter and tried to flee to safety to the mountains of Edom, were not protected but handed over to the enemy, "neither shouldest thou have delivered [them] up."

This vision clearly exposes, without mercy, without any makeup, Edom's brutality, which was the natural result of pride.

## Pride in the Church

We need to stop here and analyze this sin in the church today. Meekness and humility is looked down upon; brutality and oppression of the poor is defined as prosperity and the "blessing of God." To be something or somebody, to be proud of one's self, family, and nation is not only accepted but encouraged in the church today. When the Apostle Paul writes to his spiritual son Timothy, he specifically emphasizes that it will be worse in the end stages of the end times: "This know also, that in the last days perilous times shall come" (2 Timothy 3:1). Then

20

he enumerates 18 characteristics of religious people within Churchianity who call themselves Christians: "For men shall be lovers of their own selves, covetous, boasters, proud, blasphemers, disobedient to parents, unthankful, unholy, Without natural affection, trucebreakers, false accusers, incontinent, fierce, despisers of those that are good, Traitors, heady, highminded, lovers of pleasures more than lovers of God" (verses 2-4). These are not atheists, Muslims, Hindus, etc; this speaks of people in the midst of the church (see verse 5).

Is it true that you are full of self-esteem, a lover of self, a boaster, and proud? Is it possible that you are a lover of pleasures more than a lover of God? No one can answer these questions except yourself.

Note also that verse 5 confirms that these are religious people: "Having a form of godliness, but denying the power thereof: from such turn away." What power are they denying? The power of turning a sinner into a saint; the power of turning a saint into a sacrifice; the power of the Gospel to take away my rights, my self-assertion and replace it with total servitude to the Lord. That is the power of the Gospel being dimmed and denied today.

## The Heathen

The declaration of judgment by Obadiah does not exclude the nations of the world:

**Verses 15-16:** "For the day of the LORD is near upon all the heathen: as thou hast done, it shall be done unto thee: thy reward shall return upon thine own head. 16 For as ye have drunk upon my holy mountain, so shall all the

> heathen drink continually, yea, they shall drink, and they shall swallow down, and they shall be as though they had not been."

(See) Judges 1:7; Psalm 137:8; Joel 3:7-8

Both verses say, "all the heathen." That means all the people of the world are co-responsible for the evil that has been done against the Jewish people for over 2,000 years.

### Hidden Hate

Someone may now object and say the nations had nothing to do with Israel at the time of Esau. That is true historically. But in the extended sense, we know that the hidden hate against Israel and thereby against the living God, the Creator of heaven and earth, is very real today. Is there any nation on the face of the earth that agrees with Holy Scripture's definition of the borders of the inheritance of the children of Israel? Not one! All nations without exception agree that Israel must surrender Promised Land territory to Arab Palestinian settlers. What is their goal? The destruction of the nation of Israel.

To reinforce the statement of the nations' collective guilt, let's look at an example in Acts 4:26-27, "The kings of the earth stood up, and the rulers were gathered together against the Lord, and against his Christ. For of a truth against thy holy child Jesus, whom thou hast anointed, both Herod, and Pontius Pilate, with the Gentiles, and the people of Israel, were gathered together." We know that the kings of the earth did not gather against the Lord, because no one outside Israel knew anything about Jesus. Yet Scripture clearly says that "the kings of the earth…gathered together against the Lord…." Then it names persons: Herod, the half-Jew; Pontius Pilate, the Roman; the Gentiles; and lastly, the people of Israel. All, without exception, are guilty! ALL have sinned and ALL come short of the glory of God.

## The Day of the Lord

Although we may say that the "Day of the Lord" is future, because this belongs to the time of the great tribulation, I think we should allow for the possibility that the "Day of the Lord" started thousands of years ago. Why? Because this vision is not time-bound to earthly measurements or our understanding of time.

Look at an example in John 4:35: "Say not ye, There are yet four months, and then cometh harvest? behold, I say unto you, Lift up your eyes, and look on the fields; for they are white already to harvest." With this statement, the Lord demolishes our understanding of time. Farmers know that you don't go out in the field four months before the harvest and put your combine in the wheat field. But Jesus says, "They are white already to harvest." I believe we make an error if we try to sectionalize prophetic Scripture; "the day of the Lord is near upon all the heathen" was not only applicable for the past, but is also valid today. Of course, this "Day of the Lord" will continue until the climax, when the prince of darkness meets the Prince of Light.

## Dispensation of Grace

During the last 2,000 years, we have lived in the dispensation of grace. That means God does not permit Satan, who is the legitimate owner of planet Earth, to exercise his destructive intention unhindered. It is the grace of God which allows the various nations of the world to live in relative harmony with one another. It is the grace of God which allows a certain degree of peace to prevail on planet Earth. It is not weapons of war which give us the relative peace and security we enjoy, but it is His grace and His grace alone. If God were to withdraw the boundaries He has set for Satan, then no nation could function as a civilized society; we would literally experience hell on earth.

## Israel's Restoration

In contrast to all that has transpired, is transpiring, and will transpire in the future, God says:

**Verse 17:** "But upon mount Zion shall be deliverance, and there shall be holiness; and the house of Jacob shall possess their possessions."

This is very significant and greatly encouraging for every believer. We do not need to worry about what the powerful men of the world are planning; who is elected in the process of democracy; which dictator will take over what nation; or what country or city becomes most important in the eyes of the world. From God's point of view, it is insignificant; it's not even worth mentioning. Isaiah 40:17 states: "All nations before him are as nothing; and they are counted to him less than nothing, and vanity." Therefore, don't let these little, "less than nothing" nations cause you to fear or to worry—salvation comes from Zion and from nowhere else.

The nations without exception will continue to create an impressive, seemingly peaceful society on Earth, but they will all fail ultimately. In Psalm 2, we read where the heathen oppose the Lord and His Anointed, but verse 6 answers: "Yet have I set my king upon my holy hill of Zion."

## Israel Shall Possess the Land

Where Israel is concerned, God causes the prophet Obadiah to write down specifics regarding the borders of the Promised Land:

**Verses 18-19:** "And the house of Jacob shall be a fire, and the house of Joseph a flame, and the house of Esau for stubble, and they shall kindle in them, and devour them; and there shall not be any remaining of the house of Esau; for the LORD hath spoken it. 19 And they of the south shall possess the mount of Esau; and they of the plain the Philistines: and they shall possess the fields of Ephraim, and the fields of Samaria: and Benjamin shall possess Gilead."

(See) Zephaniah 2:7

When it says "the house of Jacob...and the house of Joseph," it means the literal people of Israel in the Promised Land. Fire, as we know, is stronger than stubble. Actually, it's an amazing spectacle to behold when a stubble field is set on fire; it is like an explosion. Nothing is left after the fire goes through. That's how Jacob-Israel will possess the land of Esau. That fact is also confirmed in the next verse:

**Verse 20:** "And the captivity of this host of the children of Israel shall possess that of the Canaanites, even unto Zarephath; and the captivity of Jerusalem, which is in Sepharad, shall possess the cities of the south."

(See) 1 Kings 17:9

## Final Restoration of the Promised Land

**Verse 21:** "And saviours shall come up on mount Zion to judge the mount of Esau; and the kingdom shall be the LORD'S."

(See) Isaiah 19:20; Zechariah 14:9; Revelation 11:15

The word "saviours" is translated from the Hebrew as *yaw-shah*: to be open, wide or free. These "saviours" will serve to proclaim judgment upon Esau and the rest of the world. Joel 3:16 reads: "The LORD also shall roar out of Zion, and utter his voice from Jerusalem; and the heavens and the earth shall shake: but the LORD will be the hope of his people, and the strength of the children of Israel." That alone will be true liberation. It must not be compared with any liberation we know of in the history of mankind, because this liberation is based on the

LORD. It does not come from heaven, but from Jerusalem in favor of the children of Israel.

## The Best Is Yet to Come

No other nation, city or people will be responsible for the implementation of genuine peace, prosperity and a real New World Order but Israel—Zion and Jerusalem. It is not surprising, therefore, to see the great leaders of the world expressing their unbridled hate against Zion and Jerusalem. They use camouflaged diplomatic language, which nevertheless rejects the Jews taking possession of Zion and Jerusalem and all of the Promised Land. We repeat, no nation on the face of the earth agrees with God's prophetic Word. Thus, we know we are in the end stages of the end times.

May this also be an encouragement for each one of us who believes in the Lord Jesus Christ, who is born-again of His Spirit and has become the son/daughter of God. We have a glorious future, impossible to fathom with our limited intellect. Particularly those in countries that are at war, suffering hunger and persecution; they can be assured beyond a shadow of a doubt that the best is yet to come! The question of the hour is, are you ready for eternity, or are you planning for your temporal, earthly existence?

# JONAH

*Dove*

# JONAH

| Book of the Bible | God's Directly Spoken Words (%) | Prophecy %* | Significant Names Listed in Each Book | | | | | | |
|---|---|---|---|---|---|---|---|---|---|
| | | | Judah | Israel | Ephraim | Jerusalem | Zion | Heathen | Samaria |
| Hosea | 93.32 | 56 | 15 | 44 | 37 | 0 | 0 | 0 | 6 |
| Joel | 57.70 | 68 | 6 | 3 | 0 | 6 | 7 | 5 | 0 |
| Amos | 80.95 | 58 | 4 | 30 | 0 | 2 | 2 | 1 | 5 |
| Obadiah | 97.69 | 81 | 1 | 1 | 1 | 2 | 2 | 4 | 1 |
| **Jonah** | 7.39 | 10 | 0 | 0 | 0 | 0 | 0 | 0 | 0 |
| Micah | 44.88 | 70 | 4 | 12 | 0 | 8 | 9 | 1 | 3 |
| Nahum | 40.30 | 74 | 1 | 1 | 0 | 0 | 0 | 0 | 0 |
| Habakkuk | 47.84 | 41 | 0 | 0 | 0 | 0 | 0 | 2 | 0 |
| Zephaniah | 96.92 | 89 | 3 | 4 | 0 | 4 | 2 | 1 | 0 |
| Haggai | 67.61 | 39 | 4 | 0 | 0 | 0 | 0 | 1 | 0 |
| Zechariah | 77.38 | 69 | 22 | 5 | 3 | 41 | 8 | 5 | 0 |
| Malachi | 93.80 | 56 | 3 | 5 | 0 | 2 | 0 | 2 | 0 |

* Percentage of book as prophecy according to *Tim LaHaye Prophecy Study Bible*

## Introduction to Jonah

The book of Jonah is listed as one of the twelve Minor Prophets. Yet direct prophecy is lacking. The uniqueness of Jonah lies in his audience—Gentiles. His escape to Tarshish was not in vain; the idol worshiping sailors were converted, as is evident from chapter 1:14, where their confession is to the LORD. Moreover, his message is directed to the Gentiles; that is, Nineveh. Jonah's message is immensely important for our times because of Matthew 12:39-40, "But he answered and said unto them, An evil and adulterous generation seeketh after a sign; and there shall no sign be given to it, but the sign of the prophet Jonas: For as Jonas was three days and three nights in the whale's belly; so shall the Son of man be three days and three nights in the heart of the earth." What was that sign? A prophet preaching of coming destruction.

# Chapter 1

## Introduction

The name Jonah in English means "dove." He was called by God before Amos and Hosea warned the northern kingdom of Israel about the coming invasion of the Syrians. He is a unique character among the prophets, because he was directly sent to the heathen, and he directly disobeyed the Lord. Thus, God had to intervene supernaturally in the life of the prophet Jonah in order for him to fulfill his task.

Jonah's disobedience places the Gentiles into the picture. His testimony introduced "the God of heaven" to the ship's crew. It ends with the sailors recognizing the LORD, "and made vows." Although Jonah does not prophesy, his adventure is referred to by Jesus as a prophetic sign.

## Go to Nineveh

**Jonah 1:1-2:** "Now the word of the LORD came unto Jonah the son of Amittai, saying, 2 Arise, go to Nineveh, that great city, and cry against it; for their wickedness is come up before me."

(See) Genesis 10:11; 18:20; 2 Kings 14:25; Matthew 12:41

The uniqueness of the prophet Jonah not only lies in the

fact that the Word of the Lord came to him, but also in the four words, "Arise, go to Nineveh." This is quite unusual. An Israeli, from the tribe of Zebulon, is ordered to give warning to a city that lies in darkness and sin. To tell his own people, Israel or Judah of the judgment of God if they would not repent would have been natural. But Jonah is told to go to the Gentiles, to Nineveh, the capital city of Israel's enemy, Assyria.

## God-Ordered Separation

We must recall that Israel was specifically instructed to be separated from the Gentiles. As a matter of fact, the Lord God ordered Israel to eradicate all the native people in the land of Canaan. We read in Joshua 6:21, "And they utterly destroyed all that was in the city, both man and woman, young and old, and ox, and sheep, and ass, with the edge of the sword." That was Israel's beginning, the process of taking possession of the Promised Land. From that point on, we read of innumerable wars between Israel and her neighbors. It was always about separation; every Israeli knew that they were not to associate themselves with Gentiles. That was God's order.

Now Jonah is sent to the Gentiles, to the enemy of Israe,l to tell them to repent. That didn't seem to be in the interest of Israel at all. Besides, Nineveh was a faraway place; it was way past Israel's border at the Euphrates. Nineveh is located on the other side of the Tigris River. That indeed would have been a long journey for Jonah.

## Amazing Grace

Before we go any further, I must insert an important statement that so wonderfully shows God's immeasurable grace. More than 250 years before Nebuchadnezzar, King of Babylon, conquered Judah and destroyed Jerusalem, God sends His prophet to the city of Nineveh, to give them the opportunity to repent and recognize the God of Israel. That is amazing grace!

## New Testament Segregation

Not only in the Old Testament, but also in the New Testament, we read of the strict separation between Jews and Gentiles.

When Jesus sent out His disciples, He gave clear instructions, "Go not into the way of the Gentiles, and into any city of the Samaritans enter ye not" (Matthew 10:5).

Even before Jesus was born, the angel of the Lord made this statement addressed to Joseph: "And she shall bring forth a son, and thou shalt call his name JESUS: for he shall save his people from their sins" (Matthew 1:21). No mention is made about the Gentiles.

During Christ's ministry, an unnamed woman of Canaan (Gentile), came and begged Jesus to heal her daughter, "But he answered and said, I am not sent but unto the lost sheep of the house of Israel" (Matthew 15:24). Today, we would rightfully say it was a careless answer; definitely not very polite. But this Gentile woman does not give up, "Then came she and worshipped him, saying, Lord, help me" (verse 25). Again, we hear something we would not only label as inconsiderate and impolite, but also outright brutal, "But He answered and said, It is not meet to take the children's bread, and to cast it to dogs" (verse 26). We have to understand that "dogs" is one of the lowest denominators a human can be compared with—Proverbs 26:11, "...a dog returneth to his vomit...."

In plain words, Jesus is saying that the Word of God should only be given to the children of Israel, not the Gentiles.

The story of the woman of Canaan continues, "And she said, Truth, Lord: yet the dogs eat of the crumbs which fall from their masters' table" (verse 27). This woman recognized her low position but believed in grace, to which Jesus answered, "O woman, great is thy faith: be it unto thee even as thou wilt. And her daughter was made whole from that very hour" (verse 28).

## Grace Abundantly

One of the most horrendous errors within Christianity is our failure to recognize our position. We depend absolutely and unconditionally on His grace, and that grace becomes effective when we humble ourselves to the lowest level. That means we accept the definition of Holy Scripture. Gentiles are not Jews; salvation is not of the Gentiles.

Another example is Paul. In His testimony to the Jews, he concludes with the words, "...I [Jesus] will send thee far hence unto the Gentiles" (Acts 22:21). What was the result? "And they gave him audience unto this word, and then lifted up their voices, and said, Away with such a fellow from the earth: for it is not fit that he should live. And...they cried out, and cast off their clothes, and threw dust into the air" (verse 22-23). They really got upset when Paul mentioned the Gentiles. Thus, we see Israel was well aware of their position, chosen as a special nation, separated from the rest of the world.

## Jonah Sails to Tarshish

This should suffice to show why Jonah could not grasp the order of the Lord to go to Nineveh. So, what did he do?

**Jonah 1:3:** "But Jonah rose up to flee unto Tarshish from the presence of the LORD, and went down to Joppa; and he found a ship going to Tarshish: so he paid the fare thereof, and went down into it, to go with them unto Tarshish from the presence of the LORD."

(See) Genesis 4:16; Joshua 19:46; 2 Chronicles 2:16; Isaiah 23:1; Acts 9:36

Jonah went in the opposite direction; instead of going east, he went west, to Tarshish, to Europe. He was to go by land to Nineveh; now he goes by water to Tarshish. It is significant that it says Jonah went "from the presence of the Lord."

## God's Way versus Man's Way

When we fail to do the will of God, according to His instruction, we are removing ourselves from "the presence of the Lord."

God's ways are so different from ours. We think, speculate on, even dream about doing a certain work or task we believe the Lord has given to us, but too often we fail to be still before the Lord, so we may hear what He has to say and follow His instruction. Jonah was to go east, but he went west.

## God's Intervention

**Jonah 1:4:** "But the LORD sent out a great wind into the sea, and there was a mighty tempest in the sea, so that the ship was like to be broken."

Instead of letting Jonah have his way, God intervenes supernaturally. Wind is not something we usually consider supernatural; however, in this case, it is God's deliberate act.

**Jonah 1:5:** "Then the mariners were afraid, and cried every man unto his god, and cast forth the wares that were in the ship into the sea, to lighten it of them. But Jonah was gone down into the sides of the ship; and he lay, and was fast asleep."

This must have been a mighty storm, because the actions of the sailors indicate their desperation. You don't throw out your valuables, your profit, your very livelihood, if this was not life-threatening. They knew their time had come.

These sailors were also very religious; they "cried every man unto his god." Only Jonah knew the God of the Hebrews, but he kept his peace.

## Jonah Asleep

"Jonah...was fast asleep." Doubtless, he was fully convinced that the God of Israel, whom he believed and trusted, was in total control, even during the greatest storm.

We are reminded here of our Lord, who also slept in the midst of a great storm: "And, behold, there arose a great tempest in the sea, insomuch that the ship was covered with the waves: but he was asleep. And his disciples came to him, and awoke him, saying, Lord, save us: we perish. And he saith unto them, Why are ye fearful, O ye of little faith? Then he arose, and rebuked the winds and the sea; and there was a great calm" (Matthew 8:24-26).

What a tremendous lesson for each of us. In the midst of the greatest storm, when everything seems to go contrary to our plans, when burdens threaten to overpower us and when life hangs in the balance, we may "sleep" and rest in full confidence that our Lord, who has saved us from the powers of darkness, is well able to keep us.

In this case, the storm was also for the unbelievers; they did not know the God of Israel, the Creator of heaven and earth. The sailors' lives are in jeopardy, but Jonah, who had the answer, "was fast asleep."

This is also a picture of our days: the Church collectively is falling asleep. Many no longer care about a perishing world. Urgently, the Lord admonishes us in Ephesians 5:14, ".... Awake thou that sleepest, and arise from the dead, and Christ shall give thee light."

## The Culprit

Finally, the captain confronts Jonah:

**Jonah 1:6:** "So the shipmaster came to him, and said unto him, What meanest thou, O sleeper? arise, call upon thy God, if so be that God will think upon us, that we perish not."

(See) Psalm 78:34; Matthew 8:25

Quite apparently, Jonah didn't care, but still kept quiet. So the crew had to act:

**Jonah 1:7:** "And they said every one to his fellow, Come, and let us cast lots, that we may know for whose cause this evil is upon us. So they cast lots, and the lot fell upon Jonah."

(See) Joshua 7:14; 1 Samuel 10:20; Proverbs 16:33; Acts 1:26

One thing is clear: these heathen sailors, who worshiped idols, knew something most unusual was happening. A storm of such magnitude was due to a higher power. But Jonah continues to be silent: we hear no word of testimony, nor does he volunteer any information.

This called for an interrogation:

**Jonah 1:8:** "Then said they unto him, Tell us, we pray thee, for whose cause this evil is upon us; What is thine occupation? and whence comest thou? what is thy country? and of what people art thou?"

(See) Joshua 7:19; 1 Samuel 14:43

This type of interrogation is still practiced in all countries, although today, the immigration officer or border police can gather this information from the person's passport. But in olden days, the proof of identity was the spoken word.

## The God of Heaven

Finally, Jonah reveals the most important information:

**Jonah 1:9:** "And he said unto them, I am an Hebrew; and I fear the LORD, the God of heaven, which hath made the sea and the dry land."

This was a message these heathen had not heard before: "the God of heaven."

We must keep in mind that literature wasn't widely available, and only the elite, the intellectuals, were able to read and write. The spoken word was still decisive. It was believed; it was feared:

**Jonah 1:10:** "Then were the men exceedingly afraid, and said unto him, Why hast thou done this? For the men knew that he fled from the presence of the LORD, because he had told them."

For them, there was no argument as to the truth of Jonah's testimony. They knew something extraordinary had occurred. They were convinced all was lost, and that there was no chance of surviving this most horrendous storm that had come upon them.

Obviously, this storm was different, for the sailors had experienced many storms before. Here something ex-

traordinary had occurred. These sailors were not atheists; they believed in the supernatural and were afraid.

## Jonah Judged

Next came the logical question:

**Jonah 1:11:** "Then said they unto him, What shall we do
unto thee, that the sea may be calm unto us? for the sea
wrought, and was tempestuous."

Without hesitancy, Jonah, the servant of God, who knew
the Creator of heaven and earth, demonstrates his full
trust in Him:

**Jonah 1:12:** "And he said unto them, Take me up, and cast me
forth into the sea; so shall the sea be calm unto you: for I
know that for my sake this great tempest is upon you."

(See) Ecclesiastes 9:18

This should have been very easy. After all, this man was
sleeping in the ship during a great storm; he apparently
did not care about the crew nor the ship, and now con-
fesses that he is guilty.

Because Jonah had told them he was a servant of the
God of heaven, the sailors were afraid to follow his in-
struction. At first, they hesitated to cast the servant of
God into the sea:

**Jonah 1:13:** "Nevertheless the men rowed hard to bring it
to the land; but they could not: for the sea wrought, and

42

was tempestuous against them."

(See) Proverbs 21:30

Next, we read that the sailors no longer cry unto their idols—now they cry unto the Lord:

**Jonah 1:14:** "Wherefore they cried unto the LORD, and said, We beseech thee, O LORD, we beseech thee, let us not perish for this man's life, and lay not upon us innocent blood: for thou, O LORD, hast done as it pleased thee."

(See) Deuteronomy 21:8

In fear of the living God, the sailors follow Jonah's instruction:

**Jonah 1:15:** "So they took up Jonah, and cast him forth into the sea: and the sea ceased from her raging."

We may say the sailors were converted:

**Jonah 1:16:** "Then the men feared the LORD exceedingly, and offered a sacrifice unto the LORD, and made vows."

## The Great Fish
What happened to Jonah?

**Jonah 1:17:** "Now the LORD had prepared a great fish to

43

swallow up Jonah. And Jonah was in the belly of the fish three days and three nights."

(See) Matthew 12:40

The God of heaven, who caused a storm to threaten the lives of all the men, is the same God who also caused the sea to be calm. It was He who "prepared a great fish to swallow up Jonah." One miracle is not greater than the other. God can and does on occasion use supernatural intervention for His specific purpose, even today.

Later in history, the Lord Jesus Himself refers to Jonah, "For as Jonas was three days and three nights in the whale's belly; so shall the Son of man be three days and three nights in the heart of the earth. The men of Nineveh shall rise in judgment with this generation, and shall condemn it: because they repented at the preaching of Jonas; and, behold, a greater than Jonas is here" (Matthew 12:40-41).

Jonah is highly esteemed in this quotation of our Lord. He was a man who trusted in the Lord, in spite of the fact that he attempted to "flee from the presence of the Lord."

# Chapter 2

## Introduction

The three days and three nights in the belly of a fish end in Jonah's exclamation, "Salvation is of the LORD." His prayer reveals his devout thoughts of God, the Creator of heaven and earth.

## Three Days and Three Nights

**Jonah 2:1:** "Then Jonah prayed unto the LORD his God out of the fish's belly,"

Jonah finds himself in the belly of a "prepared great fish." It is significant that the timespan is given, "three days and three nights." Quite logically, we assume that three days and three nights would equal 72 hours. Let us therefore take a closer look at this issue relating to the three days and three nights.

As already mentioned, Jesus made reference to Jonah and Nineveh. This occurred at the time when the Pharisees asked for a sign: "Master, we would see a sign from thee." The response: "But he answered and said unto them, An evil and adulterous generation seeketh after a sign; and there shall no sign be given to it, but the sign of the prophet Jonas: For as Jonas was three days and three nights in the whale's belly; so shall the Son of man be three days and three nights in the heart of the earth" (Matthew 12:39-40).

## Good Friday Controversy

Every Easter, this issue is brought up by many who insist that Christ was not crucified the day before the Sabbath. This is primarily based on the assumption that "three days and three nights" require 72 hours to fulfill this prophecy. But if we carefully follow the events of the Crucifixion to the Resurrection, we will come to a different conclusion.

In the Gospel of Luke, we read, "This man went unto Pilate, and begged the body of Jesus. And he took it down, and wrapped it in linen, and laid it in a sepulchre that was hewn in stone, wherein never man before was laid. And that day was the preparation, and the sabbath drew on" (Luke 23:52-54). That means Christ died Friday evening. The Sabbath begins at sunset Friday, the sixth day of the week. They rested on the Sabbath Day, as is recorded in Luke 23:56: "And they returned, and prepared spices and ointments; and rested the sabbath day according to the commandment."

In Mark 16:9 we read, "Now when Jesus was risen early the first day of the week, he appeared first to Mary Magdalene, out of whom he had cast seven devils." This is fulfillment of Bible prophecy: "the third day rise again." We must take notice that it does not say "after three days," but "the third day."

We also have the testimony of two disciples on that day: "But we trusted that it had been he which should have redeemed Israel: and beside all this, to day is the third day since these things were done" (Luke 24:21). They too testified that "today is the third day." The disciples knew something we apparently overlook; namely, that the Lord's death on Friday evening and His resurrec-

46

tion early Sunday morning, fulfills the required "three days and three nights." How so? Because one split second of one day/night counts as one entire day/night.

To understand this better, let us look at another example in Scripture: "For whosoever shall keep the whole law, and yet offend in one point, he is guilty of all" (James 2:10). If one little law is broken, though the person has kept perfectly the rest of the law, "he is guilty of all." Applied to the Lord's resurrection, it means that one tiny second counts as one day and one night.

Jonah prophetically demonstrated the death, burial and resurrection of Jesus Christ our Lord.

## Jonah's Prophetic Prayer

The other issue much debated is whether Jonah died in the belly of the great fish and then was resurrected, or whether he stayed alive the entire time. I would agree with the latter, because the Bible specifically tells us Jonah "prayed out of the fish's belly."

Let's read:

> **Jonah 2:2-3:** "And said, I cried by reason of mine affliction unto the LORD, and he heard me; out of the belly of hell cried I, and thou heardest my voice. 3 For thou hadst cast me into the deep, in the midst of the seas; and the floods compassed me about: all thy billows and thy waves passed over me."

(See) Psalm 88:6

Important to realize is that Jonah was fully convinced that God heard him. He calls the inside of the fish the "belly of hell," although this was not the hell of fire, but the hell of "water." He was swallowed alive by a fish.

Furthermore, his confidence is expressed in verse 4:

**Jonah 2:4:** "Then I said, I am cast out of thy sight; yet I will look again toward thy holy temple."

(See) 1 Kings 8:38; Psalm 31:22; Isaiah 49:14

He placed himself totally in the providence of God, in spite of the most horrible situation he was in.

**Jonah 2:5-7:** "The waters compassed me about, even to the soul: the depth closed me round about, the weeds were wrapped about my head. 6 I went down to the bottoms of the mountains; the earth with her bars was about me for ever: yet hast thou brought up my life from corruption, O LORD my God. 7 When my soul fainted within me I remembered the LORD: and my prayer came in unto thee, into thine holy temple."

(See) Psalm 18:6; 34:6; 130:2; Jeremiah 2:13

Jonah finds himself in the depths of the waters, in total darkness with no hope of surviving. Yet his unchanging faith in God is evidenced by his rock solid belief that God answered his prayer.

He could have prayed as David did, when he cried the words Jesus later uttered on the cross, "My God, my

God, why hast thou forsaken me?" (Psalm 22:1).

## David's Dilemma

Reading Psalm 22, one is overwhelmed by David's expression of his lostness: "I was cast upon thee from the womb: thou art my God from my mother's belly. Be not far from me; for trouble is near; for there is none to help. Many bulls have compassed me: strong bulls of Bashan have beset me round. They gaped upon me with their mouths, as a ravening and a roaring lion. I am poured out like water, and all my bones are out of joint: my heart is like wax; it is melted in the midst of my bowels. My strength is dried up like a potsherd; and my tongue cleaveth to my jaws; and thou hast brought me into the dust of death. For dogs have compassed me: the assembly of the wicked have inclosed me: they pierced my hands and my feet. I may tell all my bones: they look and stare upon me. They part my garments among them, and cast lots upon my vesture" (verses 10-18).

David prophetically foreshadows the suffering of the Messiah, whose hands and feet were "pierced" and His very garment offered for the "casting of lots."

## Jonah's Unshakable Faith

Now look at Jonah; he has no other refuge than the Lord, and concentrates upon God's residence: "into thine holy temple." What seems strange is the fact that in this prayer, Jonah does not confess his sins, failure, and disobedience, but expresses his position in the Lord: total reliance on Him.

His prayer proves beyond a shadow of doubt that

Jonah had a deep and abiding faith in the God of heaven; he had the absolute inner conviction and assurance that he would be saved from death.

This too reminds us of the Lord, of whom we read in another Psalm: "For thou wilt not leave my soul in hell; neither wilt thou suffer thine Holy One to see corruption" (Psalm 16:10). Jonah's body did not "corrupt" in the belly of the fish. Jonah is a testimony of the reality of the living Lord in word and in deed:

**Jonah 2:8-9:** "They that observe lying vanities forsake their own mercy. 9 But I will sacrifice unto thee with the voice of thanksgiving; I will pay that that I have vowed. Salvation is of the LORD."

(See) 2 Kings 17:15; Psalm 31:6; 50:14; 66:13-15; Jeremiah 33:11

There is no salvation outside the name which is above every name, Jesus Christ the Lord. Jonah's prayer presents to us a prophetic picture of being forsaken by God on the one hand, yet having the absolute assurance of personal salvation on the other.

God Himself determined the end of Jonah's three days and three nights in the whale's belly:

**Jonah 2:10:** "And the LORD spake unto the fish, and it vomited out Jonah upon the dry land."

This unidentified great fish discharges his cargo on land.

God brought Jonah back to where he started. His attempted escape to the west served to convey the power of the God of heaven to the Gentile sailors, and his three days and three nights in the belly of the fish reveal to us a wonderful prophetic panorama of Jesus Christ, "the Son of man...three days and three nights in the heart of the earth."

# Chapter 3

## Introduction

The message to Nineveh leads to repentance of the Ninevites, including the government: "Nineveh believed God."

The eight words, "Yet forty days, and Nineveh shall be overthrown" caused a nation to avoid destruction.

## Jonas Preaches Repentance

**Jonah 3:1-2:** "And the word of the LORD came unto Jonah the second time, saying, 2 Arise, go unto Nineveh, that great city, and preach unto it the preaching that I bid thee."

We already saw that Jonah, the prophet, was a person who recognized and knew God very personally. God instructed him to deliver a message to the inhabitants of the city of Nineveh.

Note the specific order to Jonah: "Arise, go unto Nineveh, that great city, and preach unto it the preaching that I bid thee" (verse 2). The city is not only identified by name, but is also referred to as a "great city." Why? Because Nineveh was considered the chief city of the Gentile world at that time.

What was Jonah to do? Preach a message that God gave to him. That message consisted of eight words: "Yet forty days, and Nineveh shall be overthrown" (verse 4).

That was indeed a very simple message. One wonders why Jonah in the first place did not obey, but rather went in the opposite direction to Tarshish, trying to escape his calling. But as we can see, in the simplicity of the Word lies the answer. We must also remember the words of the Lord Jesus. He too had a very simple message consisting of nine words: "Repent; for the kingdom of heaven is at hand" (Matthew 4:17).

## The Great City Nineveh

**Jonah 3:3:** "So Jonah arose, and went unto Nineveh, according to the word of the LORD. Now Nineveh was an exceeding great city of three days' journey."

Jonah acted in accordance with the word of the Lord. But note here again the description of the city of Nineveh: "exceeding great city." In the *Tanakh* it is translated "an enormously large city," with reference in the margin, "a large city of God." The Elberfelder translation says, "Nineveh was an extraordinarily great city," and explains in the margin, "a city great for God." This seems to indicate that the population of the city of Nineveh knew of the God of creation.

In Genesis 10, the descendants of the three sons of Noah are mentioned, and under the name of Ham, we see the name Nineveh appearing: "Out of that land went forth Asshur, and builded Nineveh, and the city Rehoboth, and Calah, And Resen between Nineveh and Calah: the same is a great city" (Genesis 10:11-12).

There is archaeological evidence of the city of Nineveh, but it does not give us any helpful information about why this city was called "an exceeding great city." How great? Let the Scripture's statement suffice, "a large city of God," "a city great for God."

### Did Nineveh Know God?

Jesus mentioned Nineveh in Matthew 12:41: "The men of Nineveh shall rise in judgment with this generation, and shall condemn it: because they repented at the preaching of Jonas; and, behold, a greater than Jonas is here." Jesus' reference to the city of Nineveh and to the prophet Jonah indicates again that the people of Nineveh had knowledge of the God of creation, the God of Israel.

Here is what Jonah did upon arriving in the city:

**Jonah 3:4:** "And Jonah began to enter into the city a day's journey, and he cried, and said, Yet forty days, and Nineveh shall be overthrown."

(See) Deuteronomy 18:22

The city's size was three days' journey. But Jonah went into the city only one day's journey and proclaimed his message, "Yet forty days, and Nineveh shall be overthrown." That was quite enough.

We may ask, why did the people take heed of Jonah's warning? Doubtless, they recognized him as a prophet of the God of Israel. This is evident from their reaction to his message:

**Jonah 3:5:** "So the people of Nineveh believed God, and proclaimed a fast, and put on sackcloth, from the greatest of them even to the least of them."

(See) Matthew 12:41; Luke 11:32

Revival swept through the city of Nineveh: they "believed God," and then acted in accordance with their belief.

## Government-Ordained Repentance

**Jonah 3:6-8:** "For word came unto the king of Nineveh, and he arose from his throne, and he laid his robe from him, and covered him with sackcloth, and sat in ashes. 7 And he caused it to be proclaimed and published through Nineveh by the decree of the king and his nobles, saying, Let neither man nor beast, herd nor flock, taste any thing: let them not feed, nor drink water: 8 But let man and beast be covered with sackcloth, and cry mightily unto God: yea, let them turn every one from his evil way, and from the violence that is in their hands."

(See) Esther 4:1-4; Isaiah 1:16; Jeremiah 6:26; Lamentations 3:29;<br>Ezekiel 33:11; Joel 2:15

The king and his nobles responded immediately to the message: "Yet forty days, and Nineveh shall be overthrown." This revival sweeping the city is now established and confirmed by the royal house, and becomes law. It is expressed with the word "let," which is repeated four times. It is significant that the king is not enacting something he himself does not do, because "he laid his robe from him, and covered him with sackcloth, and sat in ashes." This was true repentance of an entire nation.

## Waiting for Grace

The reason for the king's actions is revealed in verse 9:

**Jonah 3:9:** "Who can tell if God will turn and repent, and turn away from his fierce anger, that we perish not?"

We need to qualify the word "repent." Repentance is mostly mentioned in connection with someone committing a sin. But in this case, an entire city is meant, as we read at the beginning, when God said, "...their wickeness is come up before me." They were sinners. Subsequently, the king ordered repentance: "let them turn every one from his evil way, and from the violence that is in their hands" (verse 8).

What was the result? God's compassion was kindled for Nineveh; grace enveloped righteousness.

## Works of Repentance

**Jonah 3:10:** "And God saw their works, that they turned from their evil way; and God repented of the evil, that he had said that he would do unto them; and he did it not."

Doubtless, this was true repentance, genuine recognition of self, and total dependence upon God's grace. Nineveh did not perish, for "God saw their works." The works were the result of their recognition of God's message as proclaimed by the prophet Jonah.

How we believe is important. Hebrews 11:1 reads: "Now faith is the substance of things hoped for, the evidence of things not seen." This is an extremely strong statement. Faith, although invisible, is a substance and an evidence, which is not visibly manifested. The people of Nineveh had no visible evidence to see that this message was really from God: "Yet forty days, and Nineveh shall be overthrown." But because the people believed God, they acted correctly and the city was spared.

## National Salvation?

It seems that innumerable believers in our day try to mimic this process. They say, "America must repent," and surely everyone would agree that there is much repentance to be done. However, our country does not fit the criteria, "a city great for God...a large city of God." In other words, this period of grace Nineveh experienced will not be repeated. If we ask, "Why not?" the answer is we are already living in the dispensation of grace.

At the time of the Ninevites, Jesus had not completed His task on Calvary's cross: He did not pour out His blood for the remission of sin. Thus, life itself was a gift of God, and to be recognized as such. Subsequently, the saving of physical life from destruction was the issue, not eternal salvation.

## No Collective Salvation

During our dispensation of grace, there is no collective salvation, collective punishment, or collective blessing. Only he who believes will be saved, regardless of the nation or the family. No one will be able to stand before the judgment seat of Christ and point to circumstances, family members, friends, or nations. At that time, each and every one will be individually responsible for his or her actions here on earth, "He that believeth on the Son hath everlasting life: and he that believeth not the Son shall not see life; but the wrath of God abideth on him" (John 3:36).

We do well as believers to take the warning Paul addressed to the Corinthians seriously: "Now if any man build upon this foundation gold, silver, precious stones, wood, hay, stubble; Every man's work shall be made manifest: for the day shall declare it, because it shall be revealed by fire; and the fire shall try every man's work of what sort it is. If any man's work abide which he hath built thereupon, he shall receive a reward. If any man's work shall be burned, he shall suffer loss: but he himself shall be saved; yet so as by fire" (1 Corinthians 3:12-15).

# Chapter 4

## Introduction

Jonah is displeased and angry. To alleviate the prophet's discomfort, God creates temporary comfort, but then takes it away by preparing a worm, which killed the special gourd and exposed Jonah to "a vehement east wind."

## Complaining Jonah

**Jonah 4:1:** "But it displeased Jonah exceedingly, and he was very angry."

(See) Matthew 20:15; Luke 15:28

What was the cause for Jonah to be "exceedingly displeased and very angry"? He was a prophet sent by God; he had authority, and definitely had a close relationship with God, whom he knew intimately. Apparently, one thing he did not comprehend was that God deals with man in a very gracious manner. Surely, God could have had the message of repentance proclaimed to Nineveh in a supernatural way. Or, He could have given the king a dream so real that it would have resulted in repentance. But he chose to use Jonah.

We learn from the first verse in the book of Hebrews, that God used different ways to communicate: "God, who at sundry times and in divers manners spake in time past unto the fathers by the prophets" (Hebrews 1:1). He spoke to Joseph in dreams, to Moses through the burning bush, and to Balaam He spoke through a donkey. On other occasions, God spoke through visions, angels and messengers, but it is vitally important to read the next sentence, "Hath in these last days spoken unto us by his Son" (Hebrews 1:2). This finalizes the speaking of God to man during the time of grace.

We need to be very cautious when someone says, "God told me," or, "I had a dream and the Lord appeared." This is not to say that God cannot speak in such fashion today. He is sovereign. But based on this Scripture, He has already spoken to us, and He continues to speak to us when we read His Word. It is all sufficient for salvation, sanctification and preparation for eternity. No additional revelations are needed.

## Jonah Disagrees

Jonah, the messenger of God, did not agree with God's means of communicating the message to the people of Nineveh. He had already made up his mind. He knew that God is all-powerful, all knowing, and that He would take care of everything, including Nineveh. Besides, as already mentioned in our study, Jonah was a true Israelite, one who was taught to be separate, even to ignore the Gentiles. That was also evident in his behavior during the great storm on his way to Tarshish.

**Jonah 4:2-3:** "And he prayed unto the LORD, and said, I pray thee, O LORD, was not this my saying, when I was

> yet in my country? Therefore I fled before unto Tarshish: for I knew that thou art a gracious God, and merciful, slow to anger, and of great kindness, and repentest thee of the evil. 3 Therefore now, O LORD, take, I beseech thee, my life from me; for it is better for me to die than to live."

(See) Exodus 34:6; 1 Kings 19:4

Doubtless, Jonah was a friend of God, and his personal relationship with the Creator of heaven and earth is evident in this prayer. Yet Jonah was not pleased when God extended His grace to Nineveh by not destroying the wicked city.

## Jonah Is Willing to Die

When reading these verses, one might come to the conclusion that Jonah was selfish. One commentary actually says, "A man of the flesh." I doubt that very much because Jonah is totally willing to let go of his life, "It is better for me to die than to live." That does not sound like a selfish person but more like the apostle Paul, who wrote, "Willing rather to be absent from the body, and to be present with the Lord" (2 Corinthians 5:8).

Jonah is called a prophet in 2 Kings 14:25: "He restored the coast of Israel from the entering of Hamath unto the sea of the plain, according to the word of the LORD God of Israel, which he spake by the hand of his servant Jonah, the son of Amittai, the prophet, which was of Gathhepher." We do not know what else he said, but he was a prophet called by God for His very peculiar task.

## The Sign of Jonah

Also, we must keep in mind that our Lord confirmed the story of Jonah and used him as a sign unto Israel: "And when the people were gathered thick together, he began to say, This is an evil generation: they seek a sign; and there shall no sign be given it, but the sign of Jonas the prophet. For as Jonas was a sign unto the Ninevites, so shall also the Son of man be to this generation" (Luke 11:29-30). How, we may ask, was Jonah a sign to the Ninevites? Because he was immediately recognized as a man of God, a prophet. The words he spoke were the words of God. Pagan Ninevites recognized the difference between their idol worshiping religion and the words of Jonah the prophet.

## Waiting for Things to Come

Jonah's prayer, "O Lord, take, I beseech thee, my life from me: for it is better for me to die than to live," was immediately answered with a counter question:

**Jonah 4:4:** "Then said the LORD, Doest thou well to be angry?"

No answer is recorded, but we read of Jonah's actions:

**Jonah 4:5:** "So Jonah went out of the city, and sat on the east side of the city, and there made him a booth, and sat under it in the shadow, till he might see what would become of the city."

He found a place to rest. He expected that God would

destroy the city. Jonah had made up his mind: a sinful and wicked people deserve the judgment of God. Or, would the Lord God exercise grace and mercy? Jonah was waiting for things to come.

## God Prepares Comfort

**Jonah 4:6:** "And the LORD God prepared a gourd, and made it to come up over Jonah, that it might be a shadow over his head, to deliver him from his grief. So Jonah was exceeding glad of the gourd."

We note that God prepared the gourd, a kind of a palm tree, to shadow him. In chapter 1, we already read, "The Lord had prepared a great fish to swallow up Jonah." This was done to bring him back to land, to fulfill the task God had entrusted him with. Now we see God preparing something for the comfort of Jonah. As a result, "Jonah was exceeding glad." That is quite natural.

In the beginning of this chapter, we read that he was exceedingly displeased. He was angry because the people of Nineveh repented. The fact that Nineveh repented should have been cause for Jonah to rejoice. After all, he fulfilled his task; the people turned away from their wickedness, and repented. But that is not what Jonah did.

## God Prepares Discomfort

Now God creates something again for Jonah, this time not for his comfort:

**Jonah 4:7:** "But God prepared a worm when the morning rose the next day, and it smote the gourd that it withered."

This for Jonah should have been "easy come, easy go." He was very fortunate that this plant so suddenly sprouted up to provide cover from the sun. Needless to say, he had forgotten all about the people of Nineveh and was occupied only with his comfort:

**Jonah 4:8:** "And it came to pass, when the sun did arise, that God prepared a vehement east wind; and the sun beat upon the head of Jonah, that he fainted, and wished in himself to die, and said, It is better for me to die than to live."

(See) Psalm 121:6; Isaiah 49:10; Ezekiel 19:12; Hosea 13:15

Again, God creates something special for Jonah; this east wind was prepared to take away the comfort he had just received. He was suddenly exposed to the heat of the desert sun. We don't know what happened to the booth he had made to shield himself from the sun. We may assume that the wind took it away. Now the Lord God totally exposed Jonah in his very flesh and blood nature. Twice Jonah chooses death over life, "and wished in himself to die...It is better for me to die than to live."

What a picture of ourselves. We know the Lord; we try to do our best to serve Him, but when things do not quite go our way, we tend to give up, sometimes despairing of life. Many of us can testify to that fact.

## Jonah Dissatisfied

The Lord immediately puts His finger on the issue:

**Jonah 4:9:** "And God said to Jonah, Doest thou well to be angry for the gourd? And he said, I do well to be angry, even unto death."

Jonah is not angry for God issuing grace to the people of Nineveh, but the very plant He had just created for Jonah's comfort is the cause for Jonah to boldly and stubbornly answer, "I do well to be angry, even unto death."

This answer certainly reveals a most unusual relationship between a prophet and God. Jonah insists that he has a right to be angry. Angry about what? Angry because he lost the comfort which God had specifically created for him. This was not necessarily a selfish act on the part of Jonah, because he put his life on the line for his conviction. But what it shows is the spirit of temporary existence. We may rightly say Jonah was shortsighted. For Jonah it all seemed to be too complicated, requiring too much involvement. Here we see that God's ways are not ours and His thoughts are not our thoughts.

We often have the mistaken notion that God likes to demonstrate His reckless power over man, but quite obviously this is not the case. God desires to use man in his limitations, with his own peculiar character to do His bidding. Surely, He could have carried Jonah directly to Nineveh supernaturally, but He chose not to; He permitted Jonah to do his own thing, and so Jonah did.

## The Prophet Elijah

Jonah reminds us of another prophet of Israel—Elijah—who had just courageously challenged King Ahab and the 450 prophets of Baal and the prophets of the groves. But when Queen Jezebel threatened Elijah, "So let the gods do to me, and more also, if I make not thy life as the life of one of them [the 850 prophets] by tomorrow about this time" (1 Kings 19:2), he literally ran for his life. We read Elijah's prayer in verse 4: "But he himself went a day's journey into the wilderness, and came and sat down under a juniper tree: and he requested for himself that he might die; and said, It is enough; now, O LORD, take away my life; for I am not better than my fathers." The great prophet Elijah became shortsighted; he did not realize that God had work prepared for him.

## The End of Discussion

The book of Jonah ends abruptly with the statement of the Lord to Jonah, and with a question:

**Jonah 4:10-11:** "Then said the LORD, Thou hast had pity on the gourd, for the which thou hast not laboured, neither madest it grow; which came up in a night, and perished in a night: 11 And should not I spare Nineveh, that great city, wherein are more than sixscore thousand persons that cannot discern between their right hand and their left hand; and also much cattle?"

(See) Deuteronomy 1:39; Psalm 36:6; Ezekiel 33:11

## Amazing Grace

What these last two verses show is God's amazing grace, patience, long-suffering, and compassion for the over 120,000 people in the city of Nineveh, plus an uncounted number of livestock.

From the statement that the people, "cannot discern between their right hand and their left hand," we learn that the people of Nineveh had not experienced the judgment of God, although they were familiar with the God of Israel. They could not discern between right and wrong in relationship to God.

Reading the prophet Jonah, we are reminded of the nation of Israel. There are no other people on earth who have experienced the direct supernatural intervention of God, yet they continue to disbelieve. Jonah certainly experienced the grace of God, who supernaturally intervened on his behalf by creating a special fish to bring him back to land, by causing a plant to grow up and give him shade, but also creating a wind and a worm to destroy his comfort. Through the prophet Jonah, God shows His grace toward the Gentiles by sparing them due to their repentance. God is long-suffering; He is patient, "Who will have all men to be saved, and to come unto the knowledge of the truth" (1 Timothy 2:4).

The book teaches us that God wants to save the Jews and the Gentiles. To Israel, He gave many signs. To the Gentiles, He gave the Word; in this case, the preaching of Jonah. Nineveh was not the recipient of the law of God; thus, spiritually speaking, they were ignorant, unable to distinguish "between their right hand and their left hand." Not only does God concern Himself with the people, but also with the animals, "and also much cattle." Here we have the revelation of a loving, merciful God. What does God want from us? Nothing but simple obedience.

Friend, are you attempting to hide from God? Are you trying to do your own thing, without realizing God's eternal plan of salvation?

# NAHUM

*Consolation—Comfort*

# NAHUM

| Book of the Bible | God's Directly Spoken Words (%) | Prophecy %* | Significant Names Listed in Each Book | | | | | | |
|---|---|---|---|---|---|---|---|---|---|
| | | | Judah | Israel | Ephraim | Jerusalem | Zion | Heathen | Samaria |
| Hosea | 93.32 | 56 | 15 | 44 | 37 | 0 | 0 | 0 | 6 |
| Joel | 57.70 | 68 | 6 | 3 | 0 | 6 | 7 | 5 | 0 |
| Amos | 80.95 | 58 | 4 | 30 | 0 | 2 | 2 | 1 | 5 |
| Obadiah | 97.69 | 81 | 1 | 1 | 1 | 2 | 2 | 4 | 1 |
| Jonah | 7.39 | 10 | 0 | 0 | 0 | 0 | 0 | 0 | 0 |
| Micah | 44.88 | 70 | 4 | 12 | 0 | 8 | 9 | 1 | 3 |
| **Nahum** | 40.30 | 74 | 1 | 1 | 0 | 0 | 0 | 0 | 0 |
| Habakkuk | 47.84 | 41 | 0 | 0 | 0 | 0 | 0 | 2 | 0 |
| Zephaniah | 96.92 | 89 | 3 | 4 | 0 | 4 | 2 | 1 | 0 |
| Haggai | 67.61 | 39 | 4 | 0 | 0 | 0 | 0 | 1 | 0 |
| Zechariah | 77.38 | 69 | 22 | 5 | 3 | 41 | 8 | 5 | 0 |
| Malachi | 93.80 | 56 | 3 | 5 | 0 | 2 | 0 | 2 | 0 |

* Percentage of book as prophecy according to *Tim LaHaye Prophecy Study Bible*

73

## Introduction to Nahum

The word Nahum means "consolation" or "comfort." As virtually all the other prophets, little is known about him. Because he is called "the Elkoshite," he hails from Judah. Interestingly, his message is directed against Nineveh, the capital city in Assyria, some 100 years after Jonah had appeared there. Contrary to Nahum's name, "consolation," he unhesitatingly thunders a destructive message of judgment upon Nineveh.

# Chapter 1

## Introduction

This chapter reveals God's omnipotence and Nineveh's irrevocable judgment. Judah, however, receives "good tidings of peace."

## Irrevocable Judgment against Nineveh

**Nahum 1:1:** "The burden of Nineveh. The book of the vision of Nahum the Elkoshite."

(See) 2 Kings 19:36; Isaiah 13:1; 19:1; Jonah 1:2; Habakkuk 1:1;
Zephaniah 2:13

From the twelve Minor Prophets, two are directed exclusively to the Gentiles; to be precise, against Nineveh: they are the book of Jonah and the book of Nahum. In our study in the book of Jonah, we noticed that he had a very personal and direct relationship with God: "The word of the Lord came unto Jonah." In Nahum's case, we read, "The book of the vision of Nahum." This vision is a prophetic pronouncement of judgment against Nineveh. Jonah receives the Word of God directly, while Nahum obtains the Word of God by a vision. But, we must add, this vision is not earthly-based, but heavenly.

Nahum is not directed to go to Nineveh to speak to the people, but he receives a message in a vision; he identifies the origin of the vision—God.

**Nahum 1:2:** "God is jealous, and the LORD revengeth; the LORD revengeth, and is furious; the LORD will take vengeance on his adversaries, and he reserveth wrath for his enemies."

(See) Deuteronomy 32:35, 41; Joshua 24:19; Psalm 94:1

Note the negative connotation: "jealous...revengeth... furious...wrath." Why jealous? Here we need to read the third commandment, "Thou shalt not bow down thyself to them, nor serve them: for I the LORD thy God am a jealous God, visiting the iniquity of the fathers upon the children unto the third and fourth generation of them that hate me" (Exodus 20:5). The commandments were given to the people of Israel, whom God had led out of the bondage of Egypt; they were not addressed to the Gentiles. Yet Nineveh is different from other Gentile nations, because they had experienced God's grace.

### Nineveh, a Great City unto God

Nineveh was not brought out of bondage from Egypt, so why is God a jealous God in relationship to Nineveh? For one thing, Nineveh can be translated "a great city for God." *Barnes Commentary* says, "...God calls it 'that great city,' not in relation to its extent only, but its power. A large weak city would not have been called 'a great city unto God.'"

Also, when Jonah preached to the city, we read, "Nineveh believed God." Apparently, Nineveh had knowledge of the true God. Now, over a century later, Nahum receives the vision of the judgment of Nineveh: he declares, "God is jealous." It reveals to us that they had confessed belief in God, but had now fallen from Him. As a result, total judgment is proclaimed; it is the vengeance of God against sin and rebellion.

## God Is Omnipotent

Nahum goes into further detail, giving us a picture of the omnipotence of God:

**Nahum 1:3-6:** "The LORD is slow to anger, and great in power, and will not at all acquit the wicked: the LORD hath his way in the whirlwind and in the storm, and the clouds are the dust of his feet. 4 He rebuketh the sea, and maketh it dry, and drieth up all the rivers: Bashan languisheth, and Carmel, and the flower of Lebanon languisheth. 5 The mountains quake at him, and the hills melt, and the earth is burned at his presence, yea, the world, and all that dwell therein. 6 Who can stand before his indignation? and who can abide in the fierceness of his anger? his fury is poured out like fire, and the rocks are thrown down by him."

(See) Exodus 19:16; Joshua 3:15-16; 2 Samuel 22:8; Psalm 103:8; Micah 7:18

Note carefully, God "will not at all acquit the wicked." The general attitude is often expressed with the words, "God is love." That is true, but God is also righteous, and righteousness demands justice! He cannot overlook sin, neither can He forgive sin unilaterally. There has to be an atonement; someone has to pay for it. The Bible says there is no forgiveness without the shedding of blood.

Israel was the only nation for which God provided a temporary atonement by the blood of an animal. It is important to point out that those sacrifices did not take away sins; that blood only covered sins temporarily. "For it is not possible that the blood of bulls and of goats should take away sins" (Hebrews 10:4).

Nahum concludes his introduction of the omnipotent God with a double question: "who can stand...and who can abide" in the presence of judgment? Obviously, none can, because God is a consuming fire.

## Faith and Trust

But then, suddenly, we read of a change, an invitation to trust Him:

**Nahum 1:7:** "The LORD is good, a strong hold in the day of trouble; and he knoweth them that trust in him."

(See) Psalm 1:6; 2 Timothy 2:19

Although everyone comes under the fierce anger of the Lord, and there seems to be no escape, there is a way out: through faith in the Lord, "them that trust in Him."

## Complete Judgment

**Nahum 1:8-9:** "But with an overrunning flood he will make an utter end of the place thereof, and darkness shall pursue his enemies. 9 What do ye imagine against the LORD? he will make an utter end: affliction shall not rise up the second time."

(See) Amos 8:8

The finality of destructive judgment is revealed in the words, "shall not rise up the second time." Why not? Because there is nothing left to be judged; it's total and final.

**Nahum 1:10:** "For while they be folden together as thorns, and while they are drunken as drunkards, they shall be devoured as stubble fully dry."

(See) 2 Samuel 23:6, Isaiah 5:24; 10:17; 56:12; Micah 7:4

The prophet declares that even though the people would hold together like thorns filled with the goodness of sap—that is what it means when it says "drunken"—nothing will help. It will vanish just as dry stubble is consumed by fire.

## The Wicked Counselor

**Nahum 1:11:** "There is one come out of thee, that imagineth evil against the LORD, a wicked counsellor."

(See) Ezekiel 11:2

We realize that this speaks of Nineveh in the first place, but it is also a prophetic book and reaches into our times as well.

Note the words, "that imagineth evil against the Lord." Here we are reminded of Psalm 2:1, "Why do the heathen rage, and the people imagine a vain thing?" What is the aim of their imagination? Verse 2 gives the answer, "against the LORD, and against his anointed." That is always the ultimate rebellion; it is the revelation of direct inspiration from Lucifer, who rebelled against the God of heaven. He said, "I will ascend above the heights of the clouds; I will be like the most High" (Isaiah 14:14).

Some assume that the Antichrist must come out of Nineveh because of this verse. But I think this is showing the collective rebellion of Nineveh, initiated by the "wicked counselor" against the God of heaven. This is a conspiracy by the father of rebellion, Satan himself.

We can see this in another example in Ezekiel 28, where the prophet addresses a lamentation against "the king of Tyrus" in verse 12. But when we continue to read, Lucifer is revealed. Note verse 15, "Thou wast perfect in thy ways from the day that thou wast created, till iniquity was found in thee." Obviously, this does not speak of the king of Tyrus, because he was never "perfect in his ways"; neither was he "the anointed cherub," as it says in verse 14. This is a revelation of the god of this world, Satan.

## No More Grace
This prophecy is directed against Nineveh; there is no

more grace, no point of return:

**Nahum 1:12:** "Thus saith the LORD; Though they be quiet, and likewise many, yet thus shall they be cut down, when he shall pass through. Though I have afflicted thee, I will afflict thee no more."

(See) Isaiah 10:33-34

"I will afflict thee no more" means that there is nothing left to afflict.

## Break the Yoke

The next verse seems to give a positive light, but in reality, it does not:

**Nahum 1:13:** "For now will I break his yoke from off thee, and will burst thy bonds in sunder."

(See) Isaiah 9:4; 10:27; Jeremiah 2:20

It is the yoke and the bonds of God's limits, which He has set for the nations. Here Psalm 2:3 gives us another clue, "Let us break their bands asunder, and cast away their cords from us." The nations want to be liberated. That is why they try to break the "bands" and cast away the "cords" of the law of God, revealed in the principles of the Ten Commandments. Man is creating his own law, the law of freedom and liberty according to his wicked heart.

## End Announced

One more time, very specifically and insistently, judgment is proclaimed upon Nineveh:

> **Nahum 1:14:** "And the LORD hath given a commandment concerning thee, that no more of thy name be sown: out of the house of thy gods will I cut off the graven image and the molten image: I will make thy grave; for thou art vile."

(See) Job 18:17; Psalm 109:13; Isaiah 14:22; Micah 5:13-14

The words, "no more of thy name be sown" spell the ultimate end. No seed means no harvest, no food, no life; death is certain.

## "Graven Images"

There is no other way for God to deal with those who reject His provided atonement, "I cut off the graven image and the molten image." This surely is a prophetic shadow of our materialistic society. Most of us in the European (Western) world, do not pray to images and pictures directly, but indirectly our society worships images which are presented on the altar in virtually every home: that would be the television set, and more recently computer devices. The picture in our home dictates much of our time and resources. It presents a false future and glamorizes fornication. It always hopes for better times. For those who approach retirement age, it promises the golden years and therefore encourages hoarding riches—the more the better. But God pronounces judgment, "I will make thy grave; for thou are vile."

## Promise to Judah

**Nahum 1:15:** "Behold upon the mountains the feet of him that bringeth good tidings, that publisheth peace! O Judah, keep thy solemn feasts, perform thy vows: for the wicked shall no more pass through thee; he is utterly cut off."

See Isaiah 40:9; 52:1, 7; Joel 3:17; Romans 10:15

Here we see the distinct difference between Judah and the "wicked." This will be fulfilled only when Jesus returns. Although there is great wickedness among the people of Israel today, just as there is in the rest of the world, God in His grace will purge it, cleanse it and make a distinct and final separation between Israel and the rest of the world. "Only the LORD had a delight in thy fathers to love them, and he chose their seed after them, even you above all people, as it is this day" (Deuteronomy 10:15).

## Holy Jerusalem

From that point on there will no longer be oppression of the people of Israel. Here the words of the prophet Joel are applicable, "The LORD also shall roar out of Zion, and utter his voice from Jerusalem; and the heavens and the earth shall shake: but the LORD will be the hope of his people, and the strength of the children of Israel. So shall ye know that I am the LORD your God dwelling in Zion, my holy mountain: then shall Jerusalem be holy, and there shall no strangers pass through her any more" (Joel 3:16-17).

It is rather striking that not only will the law go forth from Jerusalem, but also "there shall no strangers pass through her anymore." Today, the nations of the world continue to express deep opposition to Israel and Jerusalem as their capital city, although often hidden. Why? The nations, under the authority of Lucifer, cannot accept a Jewish Jerusalem. That's why they established their embassies away from Jerusalem in Tel Aviv. All nations, under the leadership of Satan, will be forced to reject Jerusalem; thus, the Lord will reject them. No foreign embassy—"no strangers"—will be allowed in Jerusalem, because "then shall Jerusalem be holy."

With these facts in mind, we should now better understand why there is such fierce and even diabolical opposition to Israel taking possession of all of the Promised Land. It's not because of the terrorist or the Muslim nations; it is Lucifer himself, the god of this world. He is in charge (by God's allowance, of course). He is directing all the governments of the world. He is the legitimate god of this world. Why? Because the Bible says, he who sins is of the devil. That's as plain as daylight. Yet, praise God, there is an escape—Jesus the Savior!

# Chapter 2

## Introduction

Nineveh's end is declared with the words, "the voice of thy messengers shall no more be heard." When information is silenced, only death follows.

## Jacob and Israel

**Nahum 2:1-2:** "He that dasheth in pieces is come up before thy face: keep the munition, watch the way, make thy loins strong, fortify thy power mightily. 2 For the LORD hath turned away the excellency of Jacob, as the excellency of Israel: for the emptiers have emptied them out, and marred their vine branches."

(See) Jeremiah 51:20-23

These verses are obviously addressed against Nineveh; they are encouraged to defend themselves. From the Lord's view, self-defense is always vain because when He sends judgment in any way, shape, or form, it is final.

We take note that "Jacob" and "Israel" are mentioned. These two verses have caused some controversy among translators. Some write, "The Lord has turned away the excellency"; others, like Luther, say the opposite: "The Lord has restored the glory." Reading several more translations, the same controversy becomes apparent. This once again shows how difficult it is to translate

85

Scripture from one language to another, without losing the deeper meaning the Spirit of God intends to convey.

We need to enlist the help of the *Tanakh*: "For the Lord has restored the Pride of Jacob as well as the Pride of Israel, though marauders have laid them waste and ravaged their branches." The NIV reads, "The Lord will restore the splendor of Jacob like the splendor of Israel...."

Both Jacob and Israel are mentioned, Jacob the old and Israel the new. That means the whole of the nation of Israel will be restored. In spite of innumerable setbacks, Israel will be restored in contrast to Nineveh, destroyed.

## Nineveh a Picture of the World

While the book of Nahum begins with the words, "The burden of Nineveh," and deals primarily with the judgment of Nineveh, it also includes Israel and the nations of the world. It is a prophetic book that not only shows the demise of Nineveh, but also gives a clear picture of the future of planet Earth.

The accumulation of resources, riches, and luxury is the driving force of our "new world order": politics, money, and economy work hand in hand to bring about a peaceful global society. But we must mention that this is without the Prince of Peace and therefore temporary.

Nineveh in the end said *no* to God's Word, and the world collectively also says *no* to God's Word; thus, we can with assurance say our world is heading toward the final judgment.

Yet before it happens, Israel (Jacob) must be restored

and the Church of Jesus Christ must be completed. When the last one from among the Gentiles is added—or as Romans 11:25 reads, "until the fullness of the Gentiles be come in"—then the times of the Gentiles will have ended. From that point on, God will begin to fully restore Israel, and Israel will become the praise and glory among the nations of the world.

## Defense in Vain

**Nahum 2:3-4:** "The shield of his mighty men is made red, the valiant men are in scarlet: the chariots shall be with flaming torches in the day of his preparation, and the fir trees shall be terribly shaken. 4 The chariots shall rage in the streets, they shall justle one against another in the broad ways: they shall seem like torches, they shall run like the lightnings."

(See) Ezekiel 23:14-15; 26:10

Here we see a powerful demonstration of the armed forces of Nineveh, "the mighty men...the valiant men... the chariots...the broad ways...shall run like the lightning." But all of it is in vain, because God has pronounced judgment upon the land and the people.

This is also a picture of our days. Everyone shouts, "Peace, peace," yet they all prepare for war. Mankind wants peace, but on his own terms—without the Prince of Peace. That's why the often repeated slogan, "We are a peace-loving nation" is nothing but a bad joke.

**Nahum 2:5:** "He shall recount his worthies: they shall stumble in their walk; they shall make haste to the wall thereof, and the defense shall be prepared."

(See) Jeremiah 46:12

Even the recollection of the mighty and powerful warriors will be of no help. "Worthies" speaks of gallant heroes able to withstand any enemy, but they too shall fail.

## Destroyed by Water

**Nahum 2:6:** "The gates of the rivers shall be opened, and the palace shall be dissolved."

The city of Nineveh was situated on the eastern bank of the Tigris River, with the Khoser River running through its midst. Not only was the palace destroyed by water, but also it "dissolved," or vanished from the flood.

**Nahum 2:7:** "And Huzzab shall be led away captive, she shall be brought up, and her maids shall lead her as with the voice of doves, tabering upon their breasts."

(See) Isaiah 32:12; 38:14; 59:11

Who is Huzzab? Again, a difficult passage. Luther translates it, "The queen shall be led away captive." *Adam Clarke's Commentary* states, "Perhaps means the Queen of Nineveh...."

**Nahum 2:8:** "But Nineveh is of old like a pool of water: yet they shall flee away. Stand, stand, shall they cry; but none shall look back."

(See) Jeremiah 46:5; 47:3

A pool of water was a very positive picture in that part of the world, and so was Nineveh; but then that pool leaked and the water drained out; there was no turning back.

I was specifically struck by the words, "but none shall look back." This is most unusual because when destruction comes and one escapes, it is but natural to look back to see it, to watch it. We know such was the case with Lot's wife. She was instructed not to look back, but she did and was turned into a pillar of salt. Here we read, "none shall look back."

## "We Looked Back"

I was also reminded of the time at the end of the Second World War. My mother with eight children loaded most of our possessions onto a wagon pulled by horses, and headed to a nearby small ship, in order to escape the coming Soviet forces. Indeed, we looked back and saw our capital city Memel, glowing red with fire, punctuated by frequent explosions of bombs dropped continually by the Soviet Air Force. We looked back many times. But here, "none shall look back." Everything is submerged in total hopelessness—there is no return, there is no restoration; this is utter destruction, total annihilation. The enemies take everything that is worth taking:

**Nahum 2:9:** "Take ye the spoil of silver, take the spoil of gold: for there is none end of the store and glory out of all the pleasant furniture."

(See) Revelation 18:12, 16

Nothing is said here about the people. Why not? They escaped; they did not look behind them.

**Nahum 2:10:** "She is empty, and void, and waste: and the heart melteth, and the knees smite together, and much pain is in all loins, and the faces of them all gather blackness."

(See) Psalm 22:14; Isaiah 13:7-8; 24:1; Ezekiel 21:7; Joel 2:6

The words "empty...void...waste...pain...blackness" tell all—no need for explanation.

## Economic Superpower

Next comes the economic power structure of Nineveh, expressed by the picture of lions:

**Nahum 2:11-12:** "Where is the dwelling of the lions, and the feedingplace of the young lions, where the lion, even the old lion, walked, and the lion's whelp, and none made them afraid? 12 The lion did tear in pieces enough for his whelps, and strangled for his lionesses, and filled his holes with prey, and his dens with ravin."

(See) Isaiah 5:29

The lion is considered the king of the animal world, but the question is now asked: where is he? Where is his prey? All is gone—the accumulation of wealth has its advantages, but in the end does not help.

## Military Superpower

One more important item is mentioned: military force, the pride of the nations of the world for millennia. They too shall vanish:

**Nahum 2:13:** "Behold, I am against thee, saith the LORD of hosts, and I will burn her chariots in the smoke, and the sword shall devour thy young lions: and I will cut off thy prey from the earth, and the voice of thy messengers shall no more be heard."

(See) Joshua 11:6, 9; Psalm 46:9; Isaiah 49:24-25; Jeremiah 21:13;
Ezekiel 5:8

## Communication Silenced

There is something striking about the last sentence, "the voice of thy messengers shall no more be heard." That means communication ceases to exist. There is nothing to communicate about; it is totally void, empty and silent.

Here we are reminded of the judgment of the world's last empire, "Mystery, Babylon." When all of her riches were gone, they "...cried when they saw the smoke of her burning, saying, What city is like unto this great city! And they cast dust on their heads, and cried, weeping and wailing, saying, Alas, alas, that great city, wherein were made rich all that had ships in the sea by reason of her costliness! for in one hour is she made desolate" (Revelation 18:18-19). Then we read in verse 23: "...and the voice of the bridegroom and of the bride shall be heard no more at all in thee." No bridegroom and no bride means no children—that spells the end of a nation.

## Supersized Great Depression

What may be helpful to realize about Nineveh is that the epitome of destruction is not caused by weapons of war only, but the total collapse of all the value Nineveh had accumulated. It was a supersized "Great Depression."

The past few years have seen the global economy on shaky ground. Sometimes it almost feels like all is going to collapse, but that is not going to happen at this time. Total globalism is yet to be fully implemented. While the nations of the world depend on each other, there is still much disagreement among them, which is in the process of being ironed out. But in the end, as Midnight Call's contributing author Wilfred Hahn often says, "The whole world economy will be annihilated."

An important question: what will you leave behind?

# Chapter 3

## Introduction

We cannot deny that today's world is possessed with the spirit of desire to accumulate riches, often at any cost and in any way it can be obtained. To possess things is considered success, often misidentified with the word "blessing." Quite a number of books have been published by respectable Christian authors, insisting that material riches are the result of the Lord's blessing; thus, we should strive to accumulate more. That is extremely dangerous teaching.

The worst part is that when judgment comes, humanity collectively will not repent. This is documented in Revelation 9:20-21, "And the rest of the men which were not killed by these plagues yet repented not of the works of their hands, that they should not worship devils, and idols of gold, and silver, and brass, and stone, and of wood: which neither can see, nor hear, nor walk: Neither repented they of their murders, nor of their sorceries, nor of their fornication, nor of their thefts."

## Nineveh's End

With these things in mind, let us now study the last chapter of the book of Nahum.

**Nahum 3:1:** "Woe to the bloody city! it is all full of lies and robbery; the prey departeth not;"

(See) Ezekiel 24:6, 9

93

We must point out that at the time of this prophecy, Nineveh was doing rather well. They were living in peace and prosperity, and had nothing to fear. The message, therefore, fell on deaf ears, just as is the case today.

Yet Nahum's message consists primarily of war, destruction and death.

**Nahum 3:2-3:** "The noise of a whip, and the noise of the rattling of the wheels, and of the prancing horses, and of the jumping chariots. 3 The horseman lifteth up both the bright sword and the glittering spear: and there is a multitude of slain, and a great number of carcasses; and there is none end of their corpses; they stumble upon their corpses:"

(See) Job 39:22-25; Isaiah 34:3; Jeremiah 47:3; Habakkuk 3:11

Again, we have to keep in mind that when these words were proclaimed, Nineveh, the capital of Assyria, was a powerful institution. It had accumulated great riches. Prosperity was evident everywhere, and its armed forces had conquered all the neighboring countries. They were safe and secure—so they thought.

## Witchcraft

**Nahum 3:4:** "Because of the multitude of the whoredoms of the wellfavored harlot, the mistress of witchcrafts, that selleth nations through her whoredoms, and families through her witchcrafts."

(See) Isaiah 23:17; 47:9; Ezekiel 16:25-29; 2 Thessalonians 2:9-10;
Revelation 17:1-2

Note the words "whoredoms" and "witchcrafts" mentioned twice in this verse. This not only applies to Nineveh per se, but it is also a prophecy of the future; that is, our days. Read the proclamation in Revelation 18:3, "For all nations have drunk of the wine of the wrath of her fornication, and the kings of the earth have committed fornication with her, and the merchants of the earth are waxed rich through the abundance of her delicacies." Riches are accumulated by way of *fornication*; they had become rich by immoral ways and means.

In 2008, shockwaves rattled the world. Banks went bankrupt; others had to be rescued by the government. The stock market went into a semi-depression, and the experts of the world were at a loss to answer the simple question: why? No one had a real answer. A few years later, when the economy got some wind, everything was forgotten. Today, we know it was only a foreshadowing of things to come.

## Nothing but Judgment

**Nahum 3:5-6:** "Behold, I am against thee, saith the LORD of hosts; and I will discover thy skirts upon thy face, and I will show the nations thy nakedness, and the kingdoms thy shame. 6 And I will cast abominable filth upon thee, and make thee vile, and will set thee as a gazingstock."

(See) Isaiah 47:2-3; Jeremiah 13:26; Ezekiel 16:37

Here the truth is finally revealed. Truth does not spare, but exposes all. There will be no cover-up, no hiding, no camouflaging.

### Safety in His Word

Blessed is he who permits the Word of God to judge him now, "For the word of God is quick, and powerful, and sharper than any twoedged sword, piercing even to the dividing asunder of soul and spirit, and of the joints and marrow, and is a discerner of the thoughts and intents of the heart" (Hebrews 4:12).

### No Hope, No Comfort

**Nahum 3:7-8:** "And it shall come to pass, that all they that look upon thee shall flee from thee, and say, Nineveh is laid waste: who will bemoan her? whence shall I seek comforters for thee? 8 Art thou better than populous No, that was situate among the rivers, that had the waters round about it, whose rampart was the sea, and her wall was from the sea?"

(See) Isaiah 19:6-8; 51:19; Jeremiah 15:5; 46:25; Ezekiel 30:14-16

The words "populous No" identify the city of Thebes in Egypt. It was built on the east bank of the Nile River, yet was totally destroyed. Only archaeological remains testify to the former glory of that city.

The prophet even enumerates the strong allies of this city kingdom:

**Nahum 3:9:** "Ethiopia and Egypt were her strength, and it was infinite; Put and Lubim were thy helpers."

(See) 2 Chronicles 12:3; 16:8; Isaiah 20:5; Jeremiah 46:9; Ezekiel 27:10, 30:5; 38:5

But nothing helped:

**Nahum 3:10:** "Yet was she carried away, she went into captivity: her young children also were dashed in pieces at the top of all the streets: and they cast lots for her honorable men, and all her great men were bound in chains."

(See) Psalm 137:9; Isaiah 13:16; Hosea 13:16; Joel 3:3; Obadiah 11

### "Thou Shalt Be Drunken"

In view of the demise of other mighty powers and kingdoms, God utters this declaration by the prophet Nahum:

**Nahum 3:11-13:** "Thou also shalt be drunken: thou shalt be hid, thou also shalt seek strength because of the enemy. 12 All thy strong holds shall be like fig trees with the firstripe figs: if they be shaken, they shall even fall into the mouth of the eater. 13 Behold, thy people in the midst of thee are women: the gates of thy land shall be set wide open unto thine enemies: the fire shall devour thy bars."

(See) Isaiah 19:16; 28:4; Jeremiah 50:37; 51:30; Revelation 6:13

As far as defense is concerned, we know that the fig tree

is not a robust tree. One cannot use its wood to make a strong building. When the tree is shaken, the fruit quickly falls off. This indicates no power is left to keep the figs.

The words, "Thou also shalt be drunken" are significant. This is a description of irresponsible behavior. We already read in Revelation 18:3: "For all nations have drunk of the wine of the wrath of her fornication." This is utter deception; it is the accumulation of riches without realizing the source. Verse 23 in Revelation 18 emphasizes, "...for thy merchants were the great men of the earth; for by thy sorceries were all nations deceived." Very plainly, it identifies today's financial-economic system: "...drunk...fornication...sorceries...deceived."

## Useless Defense

How about the mighty soldiers? Luther's translation may help: "Your people have become like women." Women were not to fight. Defense and attack were the tasks of trained men. Mockingly, the prophet gives advice to the Ninevites on how to defend themselves:

**Nahum 3:14:** "Draw thee waters for the siege, fortify thy strongholds: go into clay, and tread the morter, make strong the brickkiln."

(See) 2 Chronicles 32:3-4

Prepare for defense, do what you can, make yourself strong—but all to no avail.

**Nahum 3:15:** "There shall the fire devour thee; the sword shall cut thee off, it shall eat thee up like the cankerworm: make thyself many as the cankerworm, make thyself many as the locusts."

(See) Isaiah 66:15-16; Joel 1:4

## Bankrupt Economy

**Nahum 3:16:** "Thou hast multiplied thy merchants above the stars of heaven: the cankerworm spoileth, and flieth away."

(See) Isaiah 23:8

In today's language, the economy, the financial institutions, and the central banks will be of no help. The end has finally come.

## Leadership

**Nahum 3:17-18:** "Thy crowned are as the locusts, and thy captains as the great grasshoppers, which camp in the hedges in the cold day, but when the sun ariseth they flee away, and their place is not known where they are. 18 Thy shepherds slumber, O king of Assyria: thy nobles shall dwell in the dust: thy people is scattered upon the mountains, and no man gathereth them."

(See) 1 Kings 22:17; Psalm 76:5-6; Isaiah 13:14; 56:10, 18;
Jeremiah 51:27, 57; Revelation 9:7

It seems repetitious, but it must be said: truth will finally expose man's inability to create lasting peace, prosperity, and security. This is applicable for our times; everyone seems to strive for success, to be somebody, to secure a pleasant future. But in the end, all striving will be in vain; the end will and must come.

## Final Judgment Declared

**Nahum 3:19:** "There is no healing of thy bruise; thy wound is grievous: all that hear the bruit of thee shall clap the hands over thee: for upon whom hath not thy wickedness passed continually?"

(See) Job 27:23; Isaiah 14:8; Jeremiah 30:12; 46:11; Lamentations 2:15; Micah 1:9; Zephaniah 2:15

We note the word "continually." During Noah's time, the condition of the world was revealed with the words, "And GOD saw that the wickedness of man was great in the earth, and that every imagination of the thoughts of his heart was only evil continually" (Genesis 6:5).

## The World Destroyed?

In view of this shocking pronouncement of judgment upon the power of Nineveh, and the fact that it was destroyed, we may ask the question: what about our world, our country? Will the same judgment come upon this world? The answer is no. Why not? Because it is going to be a lot worse. Jesus said: "For then shall be great tribulation, such as was not since the beginning of the

100

world to this time, no, nor ever shall be" (Matthew 24:21).

That means unprecedented tribulation not experienced previously.

## The Ultimate Judgment

Here is the pronouncement of judgment by the Lord Himself: "For as Jonas was a sign unto the Ninevites, so shall also the Son of man be to this generation. The queen of the south shall rise up in the judgment with the men of this generation, and condemn them: for she came from the utmost parts of the earth to hear the wisdom of Solomon; and, behold, a greater than Solomon is here. The men of Nineve shall rise up in the judgment with this generation, and shall condemn it: for they repented at the preaching of Jonas; and, behold, a greater than Jonas is here" (Luke 11:30-32).

## The Ultimate Rejection

At the coming of Emmanuel, Israel refused repentance. John the Baptist prepared the way for the Lord with a very short gospel message: "Repent ye: for the kingdom of heaven is at hand" (Matthew 3:2). In the next chapter, we read of Jesus repeating the message, challenging Israel, "Repent: for the kingdom of heaven is at hand" (Matthew 4:17). Israel did not repent. Isaiah's prophecy was fulfilled, "Make the heart of this people fat, and make their ears heavy, and shut their eyes; lest they see with their eyes, and hear with their ears, and understand with their heart, and convert, and be healed" (Isaiah 6:10).

## What about Today?

Based on the clear documentation we have in Scripture, it is going to get worse. Why? Because God has granted His grace for 2,000 years, and collectively, the world has rejected salvation in Christ Jesus. That's why our world does not have a future.

But blessed is he who has separated himself from this world, and trusts exclusively in the redemption Christ accomplished on Calvary's cross. Such a one is practicing Titus 2:13: "Looking for that blessed hope, and the glorious appearing of the great God and our Savior Jesus Christ."

# HABAKKUK

*Embrace*

# HABAKKUK

| Book of the Bible | God's Directly Spoken Words (%) | Prophecy %* | Significant Names Listed in Each Book | | | | | | |
|---|---|---|---|---|---|---|---|---|---|
| | | | Judah | Israel | Ephraim | Jerusalem | Zion | Heathen | Samaria |
| Hosea | 93.32 | 56 | 15 | 44 | 37 | 0 | 0 | 0 | 6 |
| Joel | 57.70 | 68 | 6 | 3 | 0 | 6 | 7 | 5 | 0 |
| Amos | 80.95 | 58 | 4 | 30 | 0 | 2 | 2 | 1 | 5 |
| Obadiah | 97.69 | 81 | 1 | 1 | 1 | 2 | 2 | 4 | 1 |
| Jonah | 7.39 | 10 | 0 | 0 | 0 | 0 | 0 | 0 | 0 |
| Micah | 44.88 | 70 | 4 | 12 | 0 | 8 | 9 | 1 | 3 |
| Nahum | 40.30 | 74 | 1 | 1 | 0 | 0 | 0 | 0 | 0 |
| Habakkuk | 47.84 | 41 | 0 | 0 | 0 | 0 | 0 | 2 | 0 |
| Zephaniah | 96.92 | 89 | 3 | 4 | 0 | 4 | 2 | 1 | 0 |
| Haggai | 67.61 | 39 | 4 | 0 | 0 | 0 | 0 | 1 | 0 |
| Zechariah | 77.38 | 69 | 22 | 5 | 3 | 41 | 8 | 5 | 0 |
| Malachi | 93.80 | 56 | 3 | 5 | 0 | 2 | 0 | 2 | 0 |

\* Percentage of book as prophecy according to *Tim LaHaye Prophecy Study Bible*

## Introduction to Habakkuk

In English, Habakkuk means "embrace." This book appears shortly before the Chaldeans execute judgment upon Judah. Habakkuk is considered the prayer warrior among the prophets. His direct address in the form of questions reveals his deep, unshakeable faith, which is highlighted with the words, "The just shall live by his faith." In answer to Habakkuk's prayer, God utters important prophecies which reach into our time.

## Chapter 1

### Introduction

Habakkuk is often called the praying prophet. He sees the destructive power of the Chaldeans, and prophetically reveals Antichrist with the words,, "his power unto his god." Daniel confirms this, "...honor the god of forces" (Daniel 11:38).

### The Burden of Habakkuk

**Habakkuk 1:1:** "The burden which Habakkuk the prophet did see."

(See) Isaiah 13:1; Nahum 1:1

Among the 12 Minor Prophets, Habakkuk is unusual. This is expressed with the introduction: "The burden which Habakkuk the prophet did see" (verse 1). Obviously, this is spiritually prophetic; it relates to heaven as well as the earth. Habakkuk was a servant of God who was in touch with God. This becomes obvious when we read the last chapter of his book, "A prayer of Habakkuk the prophet..." (Habakkuk 3:1).

### Unanswered Prayer

Instead of showing us events to come, Habakkuk asks some vital questions directly to the Lord:

**Habakkuk 1:2-3:** "O LORD, how long shall I cry, and thou wilt not hear! even cry out unto thee of violence, and thou wilt not save! 3 Why dost thou show me iniquity, and cause me to behold grievance? for spoiling and violence are before me: and there are that raise up strife and contention."

(See) Psalm 13:1-2; 22:1-2; 55:9-11; Jeremiah 15:10; 2 Peter 2:8

The prophet is overwhelmed by what he sees, "iniquity... spoiling...violence...strife...contention." Yet the Lord does not give him an answer: He is silent. Habakkuk makes his case when he says, "and thou wilt not save!"

Whose iniquity is God showing him? It is the iniquity of Judah. Luther translates the last words of verse 3: "Violence supercedes judgment." The *Tenakh* reads: "Judgment emerges deformed."

**Habakkuk 1:4:** "Therefore the law is slacked, and judgment doth never go forth: for the wicked doth compass about the righteous; therefore wrong judgment proceedeth."

(See) Job 12:6; Psalm 12:8; 58:1, 2; Ezekiel 9:9

This concerns Judah, because the 10-tribe Israel has already been defeated and led into captivity to foreign lands. Although it doesn't say Judah, we know the identity because the enemy who will judge Judah is the Chaldeans.

## The Coming Messiah Proclaimed

**Habakkuk 1:5:** "Behold ye among the heathen, and regard, and wonder marvellously: for I will work a work in your days, which ye will not believe, though it be told you."

(See) Isaiah 29:14; Acts 13:41

This verse almost seems as if it is out of context. But when we read the entire book of Habakkuk, we realize it is not. In the midst of greatest discouragement and severest judgment, there is a message of hope.

The Apostle Paul on his missionary journey comes to Antioch and preaches in the synagogue, confirming that prophecy is being fulfilled. Acts 13:39 reads: "And by him all that believe are justified from all things, from which ye could not be justified by the law of Moses." Then he gives a serious warning, using Habakkuk's words: "Beware therefore, lest that come upon you, which is spoken of in the prophets; Behold, ye despisers, and wonder, and perish: for I work a work in your days, a work which ye shall in no wise believe, though a man declare it unto you" (Acts 13:40-41).

## The Chaldeans' Judgment of Judah
Next comes the identity of the enemy who would destroy the kingdom of Judah:

**Habakkuk 1:6-10:** "For, lo, I raise up the Chaldeans, that bitter and hasty nation, which shall march through the breadth of the land, to possess the dwellingplaces that

111

are not theirs. 7 They are terrible and dreadful: their judgment and their dignity shall proceed of themselves. 8 Their horses also are swifter than the leopards, and are more fierce than the evening wolves: and their horsemen shall spread themselves, and their horsemen shall come from far; they shall fly as the eagle that hasteth to eat. 9 They shall come all for violence: their faces shall sup up as the east wind, and they shall gather the captivity as the sand. 10 And they shall scoff at the kings, and the princes shall be a scorn unto them: they shall deride every strong hold; for they shall heap dust, and take it."

(See) Deuteronomy 28:49-50; 2 Kings 24:2; Jeremiah 4:11-13

Many translations use the word Babylon instead of Chaldeans. We know that the Chaldeans are also identified as Babylonians. Daniel chapter 5 identifies Nebuchadnezzar as the father of Belshazzar, king of the Chaldeans. Verse 18 reads: "O thou king, the most high God gave Nebuchadnezzar thy father a kingdom, and majesty, and glory, and honour." In verse 30 it says, "In that night was Belshazzar the king of the Chaldeans slain." In this case, the words "Babylon" and "Chaldean" may be interchanged. Reading this reveals the power of Babylon's military force. There was no opposing them; they marched from victory to victory with overwhelming force.

## Prophecy of Our Times
While this speaks of the Babylonian enemy, we have sufficient reason to believe that it also speaks of the

end times.

For example, Daniel 7:7, "After this I saw in the night visions, and behold a fourth beast, dreadful and terrible, and strong exceedingly; and it had great iron teeth: it devoured and brake in pieces, and stamped the residue with the feet of it: and it was diverse from all the beasts that were before it; and it had ten horns." Here we have the "dreadful" and "terrible" last Gentile world empire. During Babylonian times, this empire was limited to the Mid-East, but the last one is truly global. The words, "breadth of the land" in Habakkuk 1:6, Luther translates, "all of the earth"; the NIV reads, "who sweep across the whole earth." We must therefore come to the conclusion that this prophecy was not limited to the literal Babylonian Empire, but incorporates the last one, "Mystery Babylon" in Revelation 17:5.

Especially in our days, we are witnessing the rise of a global world. This was made painfully clear during the worldwide financial meltdown in 2008, resulting in the closing of many banks. Innumerable businesses, considered to be rock solid investments, ended up bankrupt. Now, for the first time in history, a truly global world is becoming more and more a reality.

## New Age Powers

"And they shall scoff at the kings, and the princes shall be a scorn unto them" (verse 10).

Literally, kings or governments in our days have been reduced to symbolic figures. The people are in charge;

they indeed "scoff" at authority. The superpowers of our days, if we may call them so, are no longer based on one leader's authority but have become a mixture of communism, socialism, and democracy. For example, communist China at this time is the "rich uncle" of the world. Socialist Europe is the economic-political powerhouse. This new political mixture has flooded planet Earth, and there is no return. No civilized country can function properly without utilizing capitalism, socialism, and communism—that is an irreversible fact.

## The Fatal Mistake

There is one fatal mistake Babylon made, and it is being repeated by today's modern Babylon. It is revealed in the next verse:

**Habakkuk 1:11:** "Then shall his mind change, and he shall pass over, and offend, imputing this his power unto his god."

(See) Daniel 4:30

Here we see the power of Antichrist revealed, the one who will change his mind and break the covenant: "Yea, he magnified himself even to the prince of the host, and by him the daily sacrifice was taken away, and the place of his sanctuary was cast down...And the king shall do according to his will; and he shall exalt himself, and magnify himself above every god, and shall speak marvellous things against the God of gods, and shall prosper till the indignation be accomplished: for that that is determined

114

shall be done" (Daniel 8:11; 11:36).

## Double Fulfillment

On the one hand, we see that this was fulfilled in King Nebuchadnezzar, who gives us his testimony in Daniel 4:30: "The king spake, and said, Is not this great Babylon, that I have built for the house of the kingdom by the might of my power, and for the honour of my majesty?" On the other hand, however, it is yet to be fulfilled under the auspices of Mystery Babylon, the global world. Here is the description the Apostle Paul gives in 2 Thessalonians 2:4: 'Who opposeth and exalteth himself above all that is called God, or that is worshipped; so that he as God sitteth in the temple of God, showing himself that he is God."

## The Everlasting Revealed

Immediately after this horrible picture was revealed to Habakkuk, we read:

**Habakkuk 1:12:** "Art thou not from everlasting, O LORD my God, mine Holy One? we shall not die. O LORD, thou hast ordained them for judgment; and, O mighty God, thou hast established them for correction."

(See) Deuteronomy 33:27; Psalm 90:2; Malachi 3:6

In response to the threatened total annihilation of Judah by the Chaldeans, Habakkuk states, "we shall not die." He acknowledges that this terrible judgment coming upon his people is ordained from God, but it will not totally eradicate Judah.

## God Is Absolute

**Habakkuk 1:13:** "Thou art of purer eyes than to behold evil, and canst not look on iniquity: wherefore lookest thou upon them that deal treacherously, and holdest thy tongue when the wicked devoureth the man that is more righteous than he?"

(See) Psalm 11:4-6; 34:15-16; Isaiah 24:16; Jeremiah 12:1-2

These statements are written in a question form, yet resolutely declare God's absoluteness. Yes, God sees everything. He is silent because He knows the limits of evil that He ordained.

We are reminded here of Genesis 15:16, where God gives His promise to Abram: "But in the fourth generation they shall come hither again: for the iniquity of the Amorites is not yet full." Sin must bear fruit, the fruit of iniquity.

## Man's Absolute Lostness

**Habakkuk 1:14:** "And makest men as the fishes of the sea, as the creeping things, that have no ruler over them?"

Man, under the rulership of the prince of darkness, the god of this world, has no saving connection to God—he is totally lost.

Here we are reminded of the words we read in Ephesians 2:12: "That at that time ye were without Christ, being aliens from the commonwealth of Israel, and strangers from the covenants of promise, having no hope, and without God in the world." There is nothing more terrible than "having no hope." Thankfully, the next verse begins with the word "but": "But now in Christ Jesus ye who sometimes were far off are made nigh by the blood of Christ."

## Chaldean-Babylonian Success

The next three verses describe the enemy, Chaldea-Babylon.

Yet when we consider extended prophecy, we recognize Satan himself, for he stands behind Babylon; he rules the world:

> **Habakkuk 1:15-17:** "They take up all of them with the angle, they catch them in their net, and gather them in their drag: therefore they rejoice and are glad. 16 Therefore they sacrifice unto their net, and burn incense unto their drag; because by them their portion is fat, and their meat plenteous. 17 Shall they therefore empty their net, and not spare continually to slay the nations?"

(See) Psalm 10:9; Isaiah 14:5-6; 19:8; Jeremiah 16:16; 44:17; Amos 4:2

This speaks of the commercial and military success of Babylon. They pride themselves in their materialistic spirit: "they rejoice and are glad." Worse yet, they are worshipping materialism, "burn incense unto their drag." They sacrifice and burn incense because of the riches they have gathered: that's worshiping the spirit of materialism.

## Our Materialistic Mind

Here we are reminded of Revelation 18:3: "For all nations have drunk of the wine of the wrath of her fornication, and the kings of the earth have committed fornication with her, and the merchants of the earth are waxed rich through the abundance of her delicacies." This clearly reveals the spirit of intoxication of material success—political, religious, and commercial.

We also see here a picture of the last church mentioned in Revelation 3, the Laodiceans, who proudly exclaimed: "I am rich, and increased with goods, and have need of nothing." But the Lord exposes the truth about that church: "and knowest not that thou art wretched, and miserable, and poor, and blind, and naked" (verse 17).

In recent years, we have been confronted by a shadow of things to come. The news media proclaimed in large letters how a financial catastrophe had befallen planet Earth. Many prognosticators saw it as a repetition of the Great Depression. But we can say with assurance that this is not the case. Why not? There is a specific reason; namely, the progressive unity of the world is not fully developed yet. When the world is truly united, it will guarantee peace and prosperity for all people. But it is a deception. Peace and prosperity can never be established without the Prince of Peace. Only He will rule and judge the world in righteousness. As believers, we know Him personally because He is our peace, He is our future, and He is our eternity.

# Chapter 2

## Introduction

Waiting for His Word reveals a detailed listing of the abominations committed. Habakkuk proclaims the Gospel, "The just shall live by his faith."

The prophet was perplexed by the things he had seen. He asked questions, but received no answer. Yet he is determined to rely on the Lord.

## Watch

**Habakkuk 2:1:** "I will stand upon my watch, and set me upon the tower, and will watch to see what he will say unto me, and what I shall answer when I am reproved."

(See) Psalm 5:3; 85:8; Isaiah 21:8

Habakkuk had not only spoken, but also he actually complained to God: "I am waiting for an answer to my complaint." He was left in the dark, with no real answer to pass on. This must have been extremely difficult for the prophet, because in the office as such, he is to pass on God's message to the people. That's what a prophet is supposed to do. He is the voice of God for the people. A priest does the opposite; he presents the case of the people to God.

Habakkuk is not a priest; he is a prophet. How was he to proclaim a message that was not clear? Habakkuk

119

does the right thing, and that can be expressed in one word: "watch."

Later in history, we see our Lord giving us the advice to watch: "Watch therefore, for ye know neither the day nor the hour wherein the Son of man cometh" (Matthew 25:13). This type of watching is not manifested in our modern day activity, but rather in a holy assurance that the Lord is coming. No matter what happens in the meantime, the key to a holy life will remain to "watch."

## The Answer

**Habakkuk 2:2:** "And the LORD answered me, and said, Write the vision, and make it plain upon tables, that he may run that readeth it."

(See) Deuteronomy 27:8; Isaiah 8:1; Romans 15:4; Revelation 1:19

The Lord simply reconfirms to Habakkuk that he received a vision from the Lord, and he is to write it down. The purpose? While running one could still read it. What is the vision?

**Habakkuk 2:3-4:** "For the vision is yet for an appointed time, but at the end it shall speak, and not lie: though it tarry, wait for it; because it will surely come, it will not tarry. 4 Behold, his soul which is lifted up is not upright in him: but the just shall live by his faith."

(See) Ezekiel 12:25; Daniel 8:17, 19; 10:14; Romans 1:17; 2 Corinthians 5:7; Galatians 3:11; Hebrews 10:37-38

The absolute truth, the undeniable reality of the prophetic Word, is that it may tarry; it may seem as if it is being delayed, but when the time comes, it will happen at once.

## Waiting for His Coming

The Apostle Peter spoke of the last days, "Knowing this first, that there shall come in the last days scoffers, walking after their own lusts, And saying, Where is the promise of his coming? for since the fathers fell asleep, all things continue as they were from the beginning of the creation" (2 Peter 3:3-4).

This is a trap placed by the great deceiver, in which many fall into these days. We hear a lot about the coming of the Lord, the end of the age, the Rapture of the Church, etc., and yet we see nothing that would relate precisely to the direct fulfillment of the prophetic Word in our days, indicating in definite terms that Jesus is coming. The thought pattern of wanting to see visible manifestation in tangible terms, lies at the heart of deception, "last days scoffers."

In verse 9 we receive the reason for God's delay, if we may call it so: "The Lord is not slack concerning his promise, as some men count slackness; but is longsuffering to us-ward, not willing that any should perish, but that all should come to repentance."

Habakkuk receives a mighty vision: with one sentence, the prophet reaches to the New Covenant, "the just shall live by his faith." Paul repeats this statement, "The just shall live by faith" (Romans 1:17).

## The Antichrist

Immediately after this glorious promise, the power structure and intention of the Antichrist is revealed:

**Habakkuk 2:5:** "Yea also, because he transgresseth by wine, he is a proud man, neither keepeth at home, who enlargeth his desire as hell, and is as death, and cannot be satisfied, but gathereth unto him all nations, and heapeth unto him all people:"

(See) Proverbs 27:20; 30:16; Isaiah 5:11-15

Note the words "all nations" and "all people." This is doubtless the gathering of the nations against the Anointed. We read of the pre-fulfillment of the gathering of the nations in Acts 4:26-27: "The kings of the earth stood up, and the rulers were gathered together against the Lord, and against his Christ. For of a truth against thy holy child Jesus, whom thou hast anointed, both Herod, and Pontius Pilate, with the Gentiles, and the people of Israel, were gathered together." It was not simply a local matter for Pontius Pilate to rule that the Lord be crucified by the hand of sinners—the whole world is involved, "the kings of the earth."

## Against the King of Babylon

**Habakkuk 2:6-8:** "Shall not all these take up a parable against him, and a taunting proverb against him, and say, Woe to him that increaseth that which is not his! how long? and to him that ladeth himself with thick clay! 7

122

Shall they not rise up suddenly that shall bite thee, and awake that shall vex thee, and thou shalt be for booties unto them? 8 Because thou hast spoiled many nations, all the remnant of the people shall spoil thee; because of men's blood, and for the violence of the land, of the city, and of all that dwell therein."

(See) Job 20:15-29; Isaiah 14:4-10; 33:1; Jeremiah 50:13

While this is directed toward the Babylonian Empire, we recognize the power of darkness standing behind it all—the god of this world, Satan himself. The Empire of Babylon indeed achieved their greatness through weapons of war and merchandise, but they also experienced total destruction. Today, literal Babylon does not exist.

This message goes far beyond the Babylonian Empire, because in the end, we find another Babylon, "MYSTERY, BABYLON THE GREAT, THE MOTHER OF HARLOTS AND ABOMINATIONS OF THE EARTH" (Revelation 17:5). Babylon was the first Gentile superpower; Mystery Babylon, incorporating all nations of the world, is the last one.

Throughout our study, we emphasize that when God speaks to a selected group such as Judah, He includes Israel and often the whole world.

## Rulers of Darkness

There is one more item we must consider: the extraterrestrial power structure under the heavens, "For we wrestle not against flesh and blood, but against principalities, against powers, against the rulers of the darkness of this world, against spiritual wickedness in high places" (Ephesians 6:12). The real enemies of the Church and Israel are the "rulers of darkness." About that kingdom and Lucifer's downfall, we read in Isaiah 14:9-10: "Hell from beneath is moved for thee to meet thee at thy coming: it stirreth up the dead for thee, even all the chief ones of the earth; it hath raised up from their thrones all the kings of the nations. All they shall speak and say unto thee, Art thou also become weak as we? art thou become like unto us?"

When Satan is locked up in the bottomless pit for a thousand years, he will meet his princes, rulers, and innumerable demonic servants. They will mock him with these two questions, "Have you become weak? Have you become like us?" That is an issue we must keep in mind when studying Holy Scripture. There is God, man and Satan. We are separated from God because of Satan, but this eternal, permanent separation was bridged when Jesus paved the way to perfect fellowship with God through His body, nailed to the cross.

### The Fourfold "Woe"

First Woe:

**Habakkuk 2:9-11:** "Woe to him that coveteth an evil covetousness to his house, that he may set his nest on high, that he may be delivered from the power of evil! 10 Thou hast consulted shame to thy house by cutting off many people, and hast sinned against thy soul. 11 For the stone shall cry out of the wall, and the beam out of the timber shall answer it."

(See) Joshua 24:27; Jeremiah 22:13; 49:16; Ezekiel 22:27; Luke 19:40

This is judgment against covetousness, which is total disregard for anyone for the sake of self-preservation. But the materialistic accomplishment, i.e. the stone and beam, will testify against covetousness; the stones cry out, and the timber confirms it. Covetousness in this day and age is the accepted norm in the business world. Without it, our so-called free enterprise system would collapse instantly.

## Our Best Is Still Vanity

Second Woe:

**Habakkuk 2:12-13:** "Woe to him that buildeth a town with blood, and stablisheth a city by iniquity! 13 Behold, is it not of the LORD of hosts that the people shall labour in the very fire, and the people shall weary themselves for very vanity?"

(See) Isaiah 50:11; Jeremiah 51:58; Micah 3:10; Nahum 3:1

We may be quick to brush off such judgment upon our own nation. But can you name a nation that was not built on blood and established by iniquity? There are none! If you have the slightest doubt about it, then please read Isaiah 64:6: "But we are all as an unclean thing, and all our righteousnesses are as filthy rags; and we all do fade as a leaf; and our iniquities, like the wind, have taken us away." Notice that this does not speak of our evil deeds or corruptness; this speaks of our righteousness! That means the very best we can offer are "filthy rags" in the sight of God. It seems that we have vastly overestimated our sense of righteousness, and equally underestimated our position as violators against the holy God.

**Habakkuk 2:14:** "For the earth shall be filled with the knowledge of the glory of the LORD, as the waters cover the sea."

(See) Psalm 22:27; Isaiah 11:9; Zechariah 14:9

In contrast to the absolute hopelessness of the world, we read of the rock solid assurance of His grace. This goes far beyond literal Babylon, even beyond Mystery Babylon, and reaches into the kingdom of God on earth, the thousand-year time of peace when, "the earth shall be filled with the knowledge of the glory of the Lord."

### Drunkenness, Violence, and Idolatry
Third Woe:

**Habakkuk 2:15-18:** "Woe unto him that giveth his neighbor drink, that puttest thy bottle to him, and makest him drunken also, that thou mayest look on their nakedness! 16 Thou art filled with shame for glory: drink thou also, and let thy foreskin be uncovered: the cup of the LORD'S right hand shall be turned unto thee, and shameful spewing shall be on thy glory. 17 For the violence of Lebanon shall cover thee, and the spoil of beasts, which made them afraid, because of men's blood, and for the violence of the land, of the city, and of all that dwell therein. 18 What profiteth the graven image that the maker thereof hath graven it; the molten image, and a teacher of lies, that the maker of his work trusteth therein, to make dumb idols?"

(See) Psalm 115:4, 8; Isaiah 42:17; 44:9; Jeremiah 25:15, 17; 51:35;
Lamentations 4:21

The words are very blunt; there is no diplomatic mincing of words, but brutal exposure of the true nature of mankind. What does drinking alcoholic beverages cause? Demoralizing exposure. Revelation 18:3 reads: "For all nations have drunk of the wine of the wrath of her fornication." The drinking of alcoholic beverages causes a person to reveal hidden things he dares not utter when sober. That is why the Bible warns us strongly in Ephesians 5:18: "And be not drunk with wine, wherein is excess; but be filled with the Spirit." Luther translates this: "Be not filled with wine, which results in a disorderly conduct."

## Endtime Message
Here the whole world is addressed, particularly the world of the end times. The prophet Jeremiah proclaims: "Then took I the cup at the LORD'S hand, and made all the nations to drink, unto whom the LORD had sent me...And all the kings of the north, far and near, one with another, and all the kingdoms of the world, which

are upon the face of the earth: and the king of Sheshach shall drink after them" (Jeremiah 25:17, 26). This speaks of the world we are living in today. Mankind loves to be deceived. Whatever the prince of darkness tells the world is quickly accepted.

At the height of the great deception, when "Satan with all power and signs and lying wonders" (Thessalonians 2:9) deceives the world, God gives His seal of approval: "And for this cause God shall send them strong delusion, that they should believe a lie" (verse 11).

## Materialism's Idols

The prophet asks questions regarding graven images and idols, which is none other than trusting our modern society and worshiping the work of our hands: the great achievements of the industrialized world, possessions; namely, indulging in the spirit of materialism.

Fourth woe:

**Habakkuk 2:19-20:** "Woe unto him that saith to the wood, Awake; to the dumb stone, Arise, it shall teach! Behold, it is laid over with gold and silver, and there is no breath at all in the midst of it. 20 But the LORD is in his holy temple: let all the earth keep silence before him."

(See) 1 Kings 18:26-29; Psalm 135:15-18; Jeremiah 2:27-28; 10:3-5, 9; Micah 1:2; Zephaniah 1:7; Zechariah 2:13

We may laugh about people who believe in idols made of wood, stone, gold and silver, but when we take a closer look at modern science and its determination that

all of creation is just a coincidence in the process of evo-
lution, we clearly see that our world indeed does worship
materials. Most people of today have much more faith
in so-called science than in the plain Word of God.

## The Technological Deception

Among the many books on my shelf, there is one titled,
*When Things Start to Think,* by Neil Gershenfeld. On
the inside cover it says, "We live in a world of increas-
ingly intrusive information technology requiring that
people meet the needs of machines rather than the other
way around." How far scientists have gone already we
really don't know, but we do know what the Bible has
to say about the epitome of scientific development, documented for us in Revelation 13:14-15: "And deceiveth
them that dwell on the earth by the means of those mir-
acles which he had power to do in the sight of the beast;
saying to them that dwell on the earth, that they should
make an image to the beast, which had the wound by a
sword, and did live. And he had power to give life unto
the image of the beast, that the image of the beast should
both speak, and cause that as many as would not worship the image of the beast should be killed." People on
the earth will manufacture a machine (image) that will
be "alive"; it will give orders and will be capable of dis-
tinguishing between who is worshiping the image of the
beast and who is not.

If we only knew the extent of the brutality of mankind
for the purpose of possessing material riches in order to
find security, then we would understand that indeed man
has began to worship materials (creation) instead of the

Creator of materials.

This chapter concludes with God's absolute total dominance, and we can only follow the advice of the last sentence: "Let all the earth keep silence before him."

# Chapter 3

## Introduction

This last chapter can be called a song of prayer. It speaks of the judgment of the nations, God's creation, and the salvation of His people. Habakkuk rejoices in the Lord and His salvation. This prayer-chapter allows us a glimpse of the awesomeness of God in a unique way.

### Habakkuk's Prayer of Confidence in God

**Habakkuk 3:1:** "A prayer of Habakkuk the prophet upon Shigionoth."

We would ask, "What does the word 'Shigionoth' mean?" The *Tenakh* in the margin says, "meaning uncertain, perhaps songs of supplication." What we do know is that Habakkuk is praying:

**Habakkuk 3:2:** "O LORD, I have heard thy speech, and was afraid: O LORD, revive thy work in the midst of the years, in the midst of the years make known; in wrath remember mercy."

(See) Numbers 14:19; Job 42:5; Psalm 71:20; 85:6; 119:120; Isaiah 54:8

The prophet prays to God to revive His works, which seem to have come to an end. Thus, revival was urgent.

131

He prays in spite of the horrible judgment, because he knows God's mercy.

**Habakkuk 3:3:** "God came from Teman, and the Holy One from mount Paran. Selah. His glory covered the heavens, and the earth was full of his praise."

(See) Genesis 21:21; Deuteronomy 33:2; Psalm 48:10; 113:4; 148:13; Jeremiah 49:7; Amos 1:12; Obadiah 1:9

It is of interest that the word "God" appears in the singular in Hebrew: *Eloah*, instead of the plural *Elohim*. This is not surprising because Habakkuk identifies geography: Teman, which is in the south of Judah, and Paran, located in the desert of Arabia. We must come to the conclusion that he speaks of the Word which became flesh and dwelt among us, because Jesus is the one and only salvation. He is from everlasting. He came to finish His work, and He is coming again.

### Heavenly Vision

This prayer is not addressed on the earthly level, for it shows the heavenly reality:

**Habakkuk 3:4-5:** "And his brightness was as the light; he had horns coming out of his hand: and there was the hiding of his power. 5 Before him went the pestilence, and burning coals went forth at his feet."

(See) Exodus 12:29-30; Numbers 11:1-3; 16:46-49; Psalm 18:12-13

Moses reports of the Lord in a similar fashion in Deuteronomy 33:2: "The LORD came from Sinai, and rose up from Seir unto them; he shined forth from mount Paran, and he came with ten thousands of saints: from his right hand went a fiery law for them." Also, we read in Revelation 1:15: "And his feet like unto fine brass, as if they burned in a furnace; and his voice as the sound of many waters." Thus, we see the prophet addressing the Lord, the Creator of all things, the great Majesty in heaven and on earth.

## The Almighty Revealed

**Habakkuk 3:6-7:** "He stood, and measured the earth: he beheld, and drove asunder the nations; and the everlasting mountains were scattered, the perpetual hills did bow: his ways are everlasting. 7 I saw the tents of Cushan in affliction: and the curtains of the land of Midian did tremble."

(See) Exodus 15:14-16; Numbers 31:7-8; Deuteronomy 32:8; Judges 7:24-25; 8:12; Habakkuk 1:12

We are reminded of the words of our Lord, "All power is given unto me in heaven and in earth" (Matthew 28:18). While verse 6 emphasizes the celestial power, verse 7 identifies the earthly aspect by naming geographical places on earth: Cushan, which is Ethiopia, and Midian, the son of Abraham, the father of the Midianites.

133

## The Lord of Creation

**Habakkuk 3:8-12:** "Was the LORD displeased against the rivers? was thine anger against the rivers? was thy wrath against the sea, that thou didst ride upon thine horses and thy chariots of salvation? 9 Thy bow was made quite naked, according to the oaths of the tribes, even thy word. Selah. Thou didst cleave the earth with rivers. 10 The mountains saw thee, and they trembled: the overflowing of the water passed by: the deep uttered his voice, and lifted up his hands on high. 11 The sun and moon stood still in their habitation: at the light of thine arrows they went, and at the shining of thy glittering spear. 12 Thou didst march through the land in indignation, thou didst thresh the heathen in anger."

(See) Exodus 14:21-22; Joshua 10:12-14; Psalm 44:2-3; 68:7, 17; Micah 4:13

Here we see the Lord of Creation revealed. He is the absolute authority, above and beyond everything that is and everything that is not seen and perceived; that is the invisible reality. But there is a specific purpose, which is revealed in verse 12 with the words, "thresh the heathen in anger." This doubtless speaks of the final judgment of all the nations, the battle of Armageddon.

## The Heathen's Rage

We have to keep in mind that Habakkuk is in prayer, united in spirit with the Lord. Thus, he passes on things which we may not literally understand nor spiritually fully comprehend. But it is clear that the revelation of the almighty, omnipotent God stands in contrast to the heathen nations.

Psalm 2:1-3 documents: "Why do the heathen rage, and the people imagine a vain thing? The kings of the earth set themselves, and the rulers take counsel together, against the LORD, and against his Anointed, saying, Let us break their bands asunder, and cast away their cords from us." We often make the mistake of identifying the heathen nations of the world as those who do not think well of us, such as Cuba, North Korea or Iran, which calls the United States the great Satan. These assumptions cause us to be shortsighted when reading Holy Scripture.

From God's perspective, there are only three groups of people: the heathen, the Jews, and Christians. The last are the ones who believe in Jesus Christ; they are present all over the world. There isn't a country void of believers in Jesus Christ. We in the USA may be more vocal in our Christianity, but that does not guarantee we have more real Christians. We may yet be surprised if we were to know the number of Christians in the Muslim world. They are not vocal; actually, they are very silent, but they are there. That is also true in China and Europe. We must never forget that Jesus says, "I will build my church," and He continues to build His church globally on all five continents. That Church is going to be completed very soon.

Back to Psalm 2: The nations of the world are rebelling against the Lord and against His Anointed, and that is why Habakkuk's prayer reveals the all powerful God in His indignation against the heathen.

## Salvation of Thy People

**Habakkuk 3:13:** "Thou wentest forth for the salvation of thy people, even for salvation with thine anointed; thou woundedst the head out of the house of the wicked, by discovering the foundation unto the neck. Selah."

(See) Exodus 15:2; 2 Samuel 5:20; Psalm 20:6; 28:8; 68:19-21; 110:6

This speaks of the people of Israel. He came specifically for the Jews. Jesus strictly commanded: "Go not into the way of the Gentiles, and into any city of the Samaritans enter ye not: But go rather to the lost sheep of the house of Israel" (Matthew 10:5-6). He came "forth for the salvation of [His] people."

In Israel, He accomplished His work when He cried out on Calvary's Cross, "It is finished." The Messiah came through the seed of the woman, as promised in Genesis 3:15: "And I will put enmity between thee and the woman, and between thy seed and her seed; it shall bruise thy head, and thou shalt bruise his heel." That is the wonderful message of Habakkuk, as he reveals in his prophetic prayer.

## The Lord the Judge

**Habakkuk 3:14-15:** "Thou didst strike through with his staves the head of his villages: they came out as a whirlwind to scatter me: their rejoicing was as to devour the poor secretly. 15 Thou didst walk through the sea with thine horses, through the heap of great waters."

136

(See) Exodus 15:8; Psalm 10:8; 64:2-5; 77:19; Daniel 11:40; Zechariah 9:14

The prophet does not reveal Him as the Son of God or the Suffering Servant, but as the One who executes judgment. It is the One we read of in Revelation 6:16, "... the wrath of the Lamb."

## The Day of the Lord

**Habakkuk 3:16:** "When I heard, my belly trembled; my lips quivered at the voice: rottenness entered into my bones, and I trembled in myself, that I might rest in the day of trouble: when he cometh up unto the people, he will invade them with his troops."

(See) Job 30:17, 30; Jeremiah 23:9; Daniel 10:8

Habakkuk saw the Day of the Lord and trembled. But other prophets saw this day also, "A day of darkness and of gloominess, a day of clouds and of thick darkness, as the morning spread upon the mountains..." (Joel 2:2). Zephaniah speaks of that day as well: "That day is a day of wrath, a day of trouble and distress, a day of wasteness and desolation, a day of darkness and gloominess, a day of clouds and thick darkness" (Zephaniah 1:15).

## Israel on Hold

Habakkuk's prophetic prayer reveals Israel's condition:

**Habakkuk 3:17:** "Although the fig tree shall not blossom, neither shall fruit be in the vines; the labor of the olive shall fail, and the fields shall yield no meat; the flock shall be cut off from the fold, and there shall be no herd in the stalls."

(See) Jeremiah 5:17; Joel 1:10-12, 18; Amos 4:9; Micah 6:15;
2 Corinthians 4:8-9

No more is said about the return of Israel and the restoration of the land, only the emptiness thereof. But that is not the end, because the prophet saw more; he saw God's salvation, and that gave strength to the praying prophet:

**Habakkuk 3:18-19:** "Yet I will rejoice in the LORD, I will joy in the God of my salvation. 19 The LORD God is my strength, and he will make my feet like hinds' feet, and he will make me to walk upon mine high places. To the chief singer on my stringed instruments."

(See) Exodus 15:1-2; Deuteronomy 33:29; 2 Samuel 22:34; Psalm 18:32-33;
27:1; 42:5; 46:1-5; Isaiah 61:10; Philippians 4:4

May this lesson be ours very personally. There is a rejoicing and joy in God's salvation. It is not sensational; it is the still small voice within our spirit that tells us, the best is yet to come!

# NOTES

# NOTES

# NOTES

# NOTES

# IIII➤ *Tap into the Bible analysis of top prophecy authorities...*

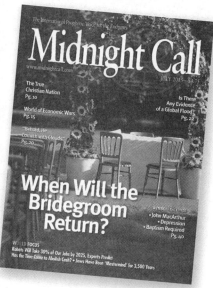

*idnight Call* is a hard-hitting, Bible-based magazine loaded with news, commentary, special features and teaching, illustrated with explosive color pictures and graphics. Join hundreds of thousands of readers in 140 countries who enjoy this magazine regularly!

IIII➤ *The world's leading prophetic Bible magazine*

IIII➤ *Covering international topics with detailed commentary*

IIII➤ *Bold, uncompromising biblical stands on issues*

IIII➤ *Pro-Bible, pro-family, pro-life*

**12 issues/1 yr. $28.95**
**24 issues/2 yrs. $45**

**Subscribe online at: midnightcall.com**